Björn Leonardz

To stop or not to stop

Some Elementary Optimal Stopping Problems with Economic Interpretations

A Halsted Press Book
John Wiley & Sons
New York · London · Sydney · Toronto

Printed in Sweden by
Göteborgs Offsettryckeri AB
Stockholm 1973

ISBN 91-20-03805-4

Preface

In the autumn of 1968, Professor Bertil Näslund, who was then my thesis advisor, gave me a sketch of a model for the situation faced by a manager who has to decide whether a development project should be carried on or abandoned. He asked me to try to make something out of it, and this is how it all began. The result is now in front of you.

This book may serve as an introduction to optimal stopping problems in their own right. The set of problems treated has been limited to a few elementary ones since much effort has been devoted to achieving clarity of interpretations and completeness of arguments and derivations. It may also be used as an introductory (or supplementary) text for students of (normative) decision making (in the fields of management science, business administration, economics or psychology) who have little experience with mathematical models and who wish to have more, since the procedure of translation from ordinary language into mathematics and back again is accounted for in detail. Only elementary calculus and probability theory have been used. Mathematical symbols and concepts follow what appears to be standard usage.

Bertil Näslund has followed my work closely and has commented on all draft versions of the main text. When he went on leave (to the European Institute for Advanced Studies in Management, Brussels), Professor Robert W. Grubbström took over as my thesis advisor. Their comments and support and those of many other of my colleagues at the Department of Business Administration have been extremely helpful to me. Ekon.D. Carl-Axel S. Staël von Holstein deserves special mention for the many suggestions for improvements that he has given me on parts of the final draft. Fil.kand. Sören Holm of the Department of Mathematical Statistics has checked the mathematics throughout and Mrs. Sylvia Mabon has checked my English. Fil.kand. Gunnel Heljebrandt who once typed the first draft of what was to become this book has also typed the last version, the one you are now reading. I am very grateful to all these people for their help and encouragement.

Financial support has been received by the Tri-Centennial Fund of the Bank of Sweden and by the University of Stockholm

Stockholm *Björn Leonardz*
April, 1973

Contents

1 INTRODUCTION

1 The problem structure 9
2 The purpose of this work 11
3 The problems treated 13
4 The mode of presentation 16
5 Other optimal stopping problems 17

2 THE BASIC MODEL

1 The problem 20
2 Translation into mathematics 21
3 Mathematical treatment 26
4 Translation back into the terms of the problem 29
5 The solution 34

3 THE BASIC MODEL WITH RECALL

1 Introduction 37
2 The problem 38
3 Translation into mathematics 39
4 Mathematical treatment 42
5 Translation back into the terms of the problem
  1 The optimal decision rule 49
  2 Properties of monotonicity in j. 50
  3 Another way of formulating the optimal decision rule 52
  4 Two questions 53
6 A more conversational treatment
  1 The characteristics of an optimal decision rule 56
  2 A derivation of an explicit expression for $v_j(x)$ 59
  3 An alternative derivation 63
7 The existence of an optimal decision rule for an infinite process 68
8 Myopic decision rules 72
9 Conclusion 74

4 THE BASIC MODELS WITH DISCOUNTING

1 Introduction 77

2 Assumptions and notation 78

3 The basic model

1 Basic results 78
2 Interpretations and comparisons 81
3 The numbers u, p, and v 83

4 The basic model with recall

1 Basic results 85
2 A more conversational treatment 87
3 An optimal decision rule for an infinite process 90

5 Conclusion 92

5 A GENERALIZATION OF THE BASIC MODELS -
- VARIABLE COST PER OBSERVATION

1 Introduction 93

2 Assumptions, notation and some general comments 95

3 Discounting and no recall

1 The general case 97
2 Increasing unit cost 98
3 Decreasing unit cost 101

4 Recall - the general case

1 The recursive relation 105
2 An outline of a derivation 106
3 The explicit solution 114

5 Recall - monotonic unit cost

1 Increasing unit cost 116
2 Decreasing unit cost 120

6 Recall and discounting

1 The general case 128
2 Monotonic unit cost - a beginning 130
3 The general case again - new notation 132
4 The explicit expressions 136
5 A concluding comment 138

7 Conclusion 139

6 CONCLUSION 142

Appendices

A1 THE TRANSFORM T_F

1 Introduction 145

2 Assumptions and propositions 148

3 T_F and a special case of stochastic dominance 151

4 Proofs 153

A2 v AND u

1 Assumptions and propositions 155

2 Proofs 156

A3 u_j AND v_j

1 Assumptions and propositions 159

2 Proofs 160

A4 $u_j(x)$ AND $v_j(x)$

1 Assumptions and propositions 164

2 Proofs 165

A5 $u_j(x)$ AND $v_j(x)$ IN THE MORE GENERAL CASE

1 Assumptions and propositions 171

2 Proofs 172

References 177

1 Introduction

1.1 THE PROBLEM STRUCTURE

Consider the following situations:

i. You want to sell an asset (a house, a share, a piece of machinery etc.) and you receive offers, one at a time, from potential buyers. How should you decide when to stop receiving new offers and actually sell the asset by accepting one of the offers received?

ii. You want to buy an asset, a house, say, and you inspect houses for sale, one by one. How should you decide when to stop looking around and actually buy one of those you have inspected (or refrain from buying a house at all)?

iii. You are in charge of developing a new product. You receive periodical reports from the laboratory where the development work is being done, telling you of the results achieved so far. How should you decide when to stop the development work and start selling the product (or altogether abandon the idea of developing a new product)?

iv. You must decide on where to locate a new factory. There are only two sites available. Before choosing one of them, you may obtain more information regarding their advantages and disadvantages. How should you decide when to stop gathering information and actually choose one of the sites (or conclude that none of them is good enough)?

In each of these situations you are facing a sequence of decisions. Each decision amounts to a choice between two alternatives, continue (wait for one more offer, inspect one more house, let development work continue for one more period, gather some more information about the sites) and stop, the last of which puts an end to the sequence (you sell the asset, you buy a house, you stop development work and let the results be commercialized, you stop gathering information and make up your mind regarding the factory sites). Your problem consists of determining the circumstances under which you should stop.

For example, in the situation where you want to sell an asset, this would not be much of a problem if you knew what offers you were going to receive. Most of the trouble with this kind of situation is due to the fact that offers appear one at a time and you can never be certain of the value of any future offer until it has appeared. Moreover, if you do not wait long enough, you may be missing a very favourable offer, and if you wait too long, the more favourable of the earlier offers may no longer be available to you. Furthermore, there may be a cost attached to the actual waiting for a new offer, such as depreciation of the asset or revenue foregone by having money tied up in it. There may also be some definite time limit, such that if you reach it without having sold the asset, you cannot wait any longer but have to accept one of the available offers. This time limit may also be seen as a point beyond which any further waiting is too costly, no matter what offers are still open to you.

Your problem is then to determine a "good" rule for stopping, taking into account

- the values of the offers you have received that are still available to you
- the availability of these offers if you continue
- how far away you are from the time limit

- the cost of the actual continuing
- your uncertainty as to the values of future offers.

For any set of circumstances (state) in which you may find yourself, the rule should tell you exactly what to do, either continue or stop. How to judge the "goodness" of a rule will be discussed later.

It can be seen that the other situations sketched above have the same essential characteristics. You proceed step by step, not knowing with certainty whether the next step will be worth making. However, if you stop, you are not going to find out what there is ahead of you, at least not until it is too late for you to do anything about it. As a consequence of this, you should not look only at the favourability of the very next step but rather at that of the whole sequence of possible future steps (by **not** waiting for the next offer, which may turn out to be a poor one, you refrain irrevocably from taking advantage of the ones to appear later etc.).

This is then a problem of sequential decision-making under uncertainty. The special kind exemplified above, where the decision to be made at each step consists of a choice between at most two courses of action, is usually called an optimal stopping problem, and that is the kind of problem that will be treated here.

1.2 THE PURPOSE OF THIS WORK

The factual situations sketched above were only chosen to point out the relevance of optimal stopping problems to managerial decision making. Numerous other examples from that area could have been listed as well, but I felt the number and diversity of those chosen would be enough to make the point of issue clear, so I stopped there. However, situations like these (having the same structure) are likely to occur in all areas of human endeavour even if they are not expressed in terms of "cost", "revenue", "sequential decision making" and the like. The problem structure is indeed a general one.

The results obtained from studies of general optimal stopping problems, general in the sense of making no reference to factual problems (apart from coin-tossing games, lotteries and the like which in probability theory play the same role as figures do in analytic geometry), could then conceivably throw some light on the consequences of various ways of handling any factual problem of the same structure. Then both the assumptions and the results of the general problem must first be translated into the terms of the factual problem in which one is interested. Since general optimal stopping problems are problems of mathematical statistics and usually treated as such, this involves the translation of mathematical concepts into verbal terms. If the assumptions seem to fit the factual situation, then the result in the form of a suggested "good" decision rule should fit it too.

However, it may happen that the suggested decision rule, after having been properly interpreted, appears to be completely counter-intuitive, even if the assumptions out of which it has been derived are perfectly sensible. You will see examples of this later. One way of getting on terms with this kind of "paradox" and at the same time reaching a deeper understanding of either the general problem or the factual situation or both, is by furnishing an argument in terms of the factual situation, an argument that shows the suggested decision rule to be at least plausible, given the assumptions (and adding nothing on the way which is very hard to avoid in a verbal argument). The mere effort of trying to find such an argument will be of help in determining the reason for the "paradox" appearing.

It is the purpose of this work to provide a clear treatment of some elementary optimal stopping problems from an economic point of view, to give interpretations in economic terms of the results obtained, and to provide arguments in economic terms that prove or at least make plausible the results obtained by other means. These other means are probability theory and mathematics.

1.3 THE PROBLEMS TREATED

We start in Chapter 2 by treating what is probably the simplest situation that still has all the characteristics of an optimal stopping problem. It is described in the form of a lottery in order to make the assumptions clear and free from any definite interpretation. The situation is the following.

You are participating in a lottery, the construction of which is known in detail. You buy lottery tickets, one by one, the prizes for which become known as soon as they are drawn. You may stop whenever you like, but you may not buy more than a given number of lottery tickets; you are then forced to stop. When you stop, you may collect the prize for your latest ticket or just leave without a prize. If you continue, you put back your old ticket among the other lottery tickets, pay for the next one and draw it. Each ticket is drawn (at random) from among all the lottery tickets. You know the cost of a ticket; it is positive and it is always the same. How should you choose between continuing and stopping under these conditions if you want to act so as to maximize your expected net gain from participating in the lottery?

Your net gain is taken to be the value of what you collect upon stopping minus the total cost of the tickets you have bought. The value of a prize is taken to be the value which you choose to attach to it. We assume that you can evaluate each prize and the "cost" of a ticket in monetary terms, and furthermore, that you want to act so as to maximize the expected monetary value of your net gain.

These assumptions are made in order to avoid a complication that might divert the attention from the structure of the problem without necessarily changing the main results (see Hayes (1969), pp 302-3). They are consistent with an assumption of risk-neutrality on your part regarding those changes in your fortune which may come about by you participating in the lottery. The alternative is to use expected utility for criterion (see e.g. Chapter 4 in Raiffa (1968) or Chapter 7 in DeGroot (1970)). The above assumptions conform to that criterion if the utility function is linear in the appropriate interval.

To participate in this lottery is then like making a sequence of independent observations of a random variable with a known distribution function, paying a fixed cost for each observation. What you need is a _decision rule_, i.e. a rule which tells you what to do, stop or continue, in all circumstances. But any decision rule will not do. The "goodness" of a decision rule is measured by the expected net gain from following it, and you want nothing but the best (in this sense). Hence, you want to find an _optimal decision rule_, one that cannot be improved; the expected net gain from following any other kind of rule is less than that of following an optimal decision rule. There may be more than one such rule but since they are all of them equally good, you are content with finding one of them. For example, the decision rule "Buy exactly ten tickets and then stop" is not optimal since it may be improved by being changed into "Continue until you have won the top prize or until you have bought ten tickets, whichever event occurs first". Essentially, to show that a decision rule is optimal amounts to showing that it always takes proper account of the value of stopping as compared to the expected value of continuing (buy one more ticket and then do the best thing), given the construction of the lottery (the distribution function), the cost of a ticket, and the number of tickets that you may still buy. We shall only treat problems for which there exist optimal decision rules.

A situation such as this is seen to have many of the properties of the problem of when to sell an asset (example i. in 1.1). It has been treated with this assumption in mind by Hayes(1969) who also considers various generalizations (see also Sakaguchi(1961) and Karlin(1962)). However, the assumption that what you collect upon stopping is the value of your _latest_ observation is not likely to hold in a situation such as the product development setting (example iii. in 1.1). You then typically have recall to any previous result when you stop. The consequences of changing the situation from one _without recall_ into one _with_ (complete) _recall_ are examined in Chapter 3. When you stop, you may then collect the prize for _any one_ of your previous tickets (you will of course choose the most valuable) or just leave without a prize. In Chapter 4 both kinds of situation are treated under the further assumption that you want to maximize the expected present value of your net gain, making use of a constant rate of return for discounting future costs and rewards. Problems of this kind have been treated by several authors (see e.g. MacQueen and Miller (1960), Radner(1964), DeGroot(1968, 1969), McCall(1965)).

All these situations share the property that the prospects of the whole future are good, if and only if, those of the near future are. This is due to the fact that neither the construction of the lottery nor the cost of a ticket change as you continue. Since this does not hold for most real life situations, we try to take account for this (in the simplest way) in Chapter 5 by letting the cost of an observation vary as you go on. Special attention is given to the cases of increasing and decreasing cost per observation. This is the most general problem treated. All the others may be derived from it as special cases. However, we have chosen to go from the simple to the more complicated.

In all cases we derive optimal decision rules and discuss their properties. In particular, we examine whether a myopic decision rule is optimal. Such a rule takes only the immediate future into account; if you follow a myopic decision rule, you always behave as if the next observation were to be the last one (see Section 3.8). For the problems with recall we derive explicit expressions for the expected net gain from following an optimal decision rule; these results appear to be new. For the constant-cost cases we also consider what happens if you will never be forced to stop. The cases with and without recall are compared in various respects.

The problems treated differ as follows:

Chapter 2	no recall	constant cost	no discounting
Chapter 3	recall	constant cost	no discounting
Chapter 4	both	constant cost	discounting
Chapter 5	both	variable	both

See the first and last sections of each chapter for further details of the problems and the results.

1.4 THE MODE OF PRESENTATION

Each problem is first stated verbally, then carefully translated into mathematics (Chapters 4 and 5 are less detailed in this respect, since the technique will by then be familiar) and solved by a mathematical argument. Extensive use has been made of mathematical induction. The conclusions are then explicitly translated back into the terms of the problem.

At first sight, some of the mathematical results seemed untenable from an economic point of view (at least to me). Economic arguments are provided for these, as much as possible in verbal terms, supporting the conclusions and often even constituting alternative proofs. A good starting point for the verbal argument (and there is a host of them to choose from) was usually found by a closer study of the mathematical formulation of the problem and of the conclusion. Thus, the mathematical arguments have served as sources of inspiration for deriving verbal arguments. Loosely speaking, "mathematical intuition" is being used to amplify "economic intuition" and to check on it as well (the other way around too, sometimes). On this issue and on the more general one of the use of mathematics in social science and economics, see Simon(1965), Baumol(1966), and Bunge(1967, Section 8.2). See Bunge (1962), especially Chapter 3, for a discussion of the concept of "intuition".

In order to facilitate the reading and the understanding of the results, the material in Chapters 2 and 3 is divided into sections so as to make clear where the translation into mathematics ends and where the translation back into the terms of the problem starts. If the mathematical results are taken on faith, the interpretations may be read independently of the mathematical treatment. Thus, the strictly mathematical parts of the treatment may be omitted on a first reading without missing the verbal presentation of either the assumptions or the conclusions. The use of mathematics is kept to a minimum in the other sections. The same order of presentation is adhered to in Chapters 4 and 5.

Some frequently used mathematical results are proved in the Appendices at the end of the book. References such as *A2P4* refer to Appendix 2, Proposition 4, which is to be found in A2.1, Section 1 of Appendix 2. By "2.1" is meant Section 1 of Chapter 2 and "4.3.3" refers to subsection 3 of 4.3. Formulas are numbered consecutively within each section; "*(5)*" refers to formula *(5)* of the same section and "*(3.5.5)*" refers to formula *(5)* of 3.5 (which is to be found in 3.5.3). Figures are also numbered in this way.

1.5 OTHER OPTIMAL STOPPING PROBLEMS

Breiman(1964 p 285) has summarized the essential features of an optimal stopping problem in the following way:

> "1. A probabilistic mechanism, that is, a random device, that moves from state to state under a known, partially known, or unknown probability law.
>
> 2. A payoff and decision structure such that, after observing the current state, we have our choice of *at most* two decisions:
>
> *(a)* Take our accumulated payoff to date and quit.
>
> *(b)* Pay an entrance fee for the privilege of watching one more transition."

In the terms of this description, the problems treated here are seen to have the following characteristics.

Firstly, the "probabilistic mechanism" is described in the form of a known, stationary distribution function; the construction of the lottery is known beforehand, and it does not change as you continue. Most real situations are not that well specified. Nevertheless you have to make up your mind somehow, taking into account your idea, however vague it may be, of the construction of the "probability mechanism" that you are facing. One way of doing this is by actually trying to represent your beliefs, hunches, and pieces of observation in the form of a probability distribution, your subjective probability distribution, and then to act as if this were to be a correct description of the situation. You will then act consistently according to your beliefs and your present state of knowledge. Given this, the assumption that you know the construction of the lottery is no real restriction. However, your subjective probability distribution remains to be assessed. See Staël von Holstein(1970) for a theoretical and experimental treatment of that problem.

But what of the construction of the lottery being always the same? This assumption has been made in order to avoid some considerably harder problems and that is the main reason behind calling the problems treated here "elementary". A typical case would be the one in which your beliefs as to the "true" construction of the lottery are changed as you continue. Even if the "true" distribution function remains the same, you will then want to revise the one you are using for a description of the situation, your prior distribution, and you will then behave as if the construction of the lottery were changed. In principle at least, this situation can be handled by the so-called Bayesian methods of statistics (which include the idea that beliefs may be represented in a meaningful way by subjective probabilities, which may in turn be treated as "ordinary" probabilities). A good introduction to this area is the book by Raiffa(1968); see also Staël von Holstein(1970) and the references therein. A treatment at a more advanced level is given by DeGroot(1970); the "classic" is Raiffa and Schlaifer(1961). Optimal decision rules for stopping problems with this feature have been found under special assumptions regarding the distributions involved (Sakaguchi(1961) and DeGroot(1968, 1969, 1970), normal distribution with unknown mean, normal prior distribution; Brown(1967), uniform distribution over an interval with unknown right-hand end-point, uniform prior distribution). However, if you have no reason to change your beliefs regarding the situation, the assumption of a stationary distribution function is still appropriate. This will be the case, for example, if the "true" distribution does not change "enough" for you to notice it. We leave this point here, but we shall return to it briefly in the concluding chapter.

Secondly, referring to Breiman's description, the "payoff and decision structure" may clearly be varied in innumerable ways within the bounds imposed. For a survey of such variations and ways of treating them, see the whole article by Breiman(1964). See also the book by DeGroot (1970, Chapters 13 and 14). The problems that we shall study share the property that time is discretized into "periods" and that one observation can always be made in each as long as you may continue. The same kind of problems have also been formulated in terms of continuous time and treated under various assumptions as to how the observations are distributed over time. See Karlin(1962), McCall(1965), and Elfving(1967).

References to the literature are only given in this chapter and in the concluding one (with a few exceptions). See the book by DeGroot(1970) for further references. The article by DeGroot(1969) has been a main source of inspiration for the choice of problems to study and for the mode of presentation.

2 The Basic Model

2.1 THE PROBLEM

You are invited to participate in a lottery, the construction of which is completely known to you. Thus, you know what the prizes are and, for each prize, you know the probability of a ticket, drawn at random, winning you this prize. You also know the cost of a lottery ticket; it is positive and it is always the same.

The word "prize" is used here in a broad sense; there is a prize for every ticket. Moreover, each prize has a definite value to you and some prizes may have a negative value.

When you buy a ticket, it is drawn at random from among all the lottery tickets. You will then know which prize it will win you and the value of this prize, after which the ticket is put back among all the others. At this point you must decide whether you want to collect the prize or not, for you participate in the lottery subject to the following conditions:

- Once you collect a prize, you may not buy any more tickets.
- If you buy another ticket, you lose the possibility of collecting the prize for any ticket bought previously.

Hence, you may collect at the most one prize, and at any time the only one you can collect is the prize for your latest ticket; you take it or you leave it.

Put another way, at each such point you must decide whether you want to continue or to stop buying tickets. You may stop whenever you like, but once you have stopped you may not buy any more tickets. Moreover, you will eventually be forced to stop: You may buy at the most (and one at a time) a given number of lottery tickets. However, when you stop, whether you are forced to or not, you always have the option of either collecting the prize for your latest ticket or simply leaving without a prize.

Your net gain from participating in the lottery is taken to be the value of what you collect upon stopping minus the cost of the tickets you have bought. At any time, the value to you of continuing or stopping is taken to be your expected net gain from choosing the respective alternative.

How should you choose between continuing and stopping, if you want to act so as to maximize your expected net gain from participating in the lottery?

Clearly a partial answer to this question is to say that you should always choose the alternative having the greatest value to you. However, in order to give a more precise answer we shall now translate the problem into mathematics. After a mathematical treatment, the results obtained will be translated back again into the terms of the problem.

2.2 TRANSLATION INTO MATHEMATICS

Suppose you are not allowed to buy more than n lottery tickets, that is, you may not continue the process for more than n periods. The process is equivalent to observing sequentially a random variable having a given distribution function. The random variable is described by the prize-list of the lottery and your evaluation of each prize; in the list you find the prize that corresponds to a given lottery ticket and your evaluation gives a definite value to each prize. The prize-list also contains a complete description of the distribution function of this random variable: you are given complete information about the probability of winning a prize of any given value.

Let the random variable be denoted by X and its distribution function by F. Then $F(x)$ denotes the probability that a ticket drawn at random from among all the tickets in the lottery will win a prize, the value to you of which does not exceed x.

If you decide to stop buying tickets when you have drawn one that will give you a prize of value x, you have the option of either collecting x or simply leaving without a prize. The latter alternative is taken to mean that you collect 0.

If you decide to go on, you must put back your old ticket among the other tickets before drawing a new one. This means that successive drawings may be regarded as independent observations of the same random variable: the distribution function is unchanged during the course of the process. It also means that once you have decided to go on, and hence to pass up an offered prize, you are back where you started in all respects except that you have one period less to go (observation to make) before you are forced to stop. However, the cost of participating has not yet been taken into account.

The additional requirement that you pay a fixed positive amount for each ticket before drawing it, implies that there is one more respect in which your situation has changed: the amount of resources that you have left. Let the cost of each lottery ticket be denoted by c, a positive real number. Let it be assumed, however, that n, the number of periods that you may continue buying tickets, is determined by you on the basis of the amount of your resources that you are willing to or able to spend on the lottery. Then n is chosen to be the largest integer such that nc does not exceed this amount. By this assumption "having one period less to go" becomes equivalent to "having c resource units less" so it will be enough to consider one of the "two" respects in which your initial situation has changed if you decide to go on. The assumption does not restrict the original problem: any procedure for fixing n may be reinterpreted to conform to it provided that the procedure is independent of the other assumptions.

Thus, once you have turned down an offered prize and decided to buy another ticket, the only essential aspect of you situation that has changed (compared to your situation before you bought the ticket that you have just put back) is the number of remaining observations that you can make before you are forced to quit. Then your situation (or the <u>state of the process</u>) before each choice of going on or quitting may be characterized by an ordered pair (j,x) where j denotes the number of possible remaining observations and where x stands for the value of the prize to which your latest ticket gives you a right. You start in $(n,0)$ for some $n \geqq 1$ and you are forced to stop and collect your prize as soon as the process enters $(0,x)$ whatever x is.

If you stop at (j,x), the state of the process is changed into $(0,x)$ and you collect your prize. If you continue, you pay c and let the state of the process be changed from (j,x) into $(j-1,X)$. As before, X stands for the value of the prize of a ticket drawn at random from among all the lottery tickets; X is a random variable, the value of which will be unknown to you until the ticket has been drawn. Thus, if you continue, you do not know which state will be the next, only that the number of possible remaining observations will decrease by one.

Suppose that the state of the process is (j,x), $j \geqq 1$, and that you are about to decide whether you are going to stop or continue. You want to choose the alternative that has the greatest value to you (expected net gain) and you want to stick to this principle in every subsequent decision regarding the process that you may have to make. Let $V(j,x)$ denote the value to you of engaging yourself in the process on these conditions. Then

$$V(j,x) = \max \begin{cases} \text{the value to you of stopping at } (j,x) \\ \text{the value to you of being in } (j-1,X) \text{ minus } c \end{cases}$$

But since "value to you" was taken to be expected net gain and since "stopping at (j,x)" means "being in $(0,x)$", the value to you of being in (j,x) can be expressed as follows:

$$(1) \qquad V(j,x) = \max \begin{cases} V(0,x) \\ E\{V(j-1,X)\} - c \end{cases}$$

where $E\{\bullet\}$ denotes the expected value of the expression within the brackets.

The value to you of stopping at (j,x) is thus equal to $V(0,x)$. Moreover, your principle of making decisions implies that you will never accept a negative prize, so if x is negative, you will choose to collect 0. Let the value of what you collect be denoted by x^+. Then

$$(2) \qquad x^+ = \max(x,0) = \begin{cases} 0 & x \leqq 0 \\ x & x > 0 \end{cases}$$

and

$$(3) \qquad V(0,x) = x^+$$

The value to you of going on when you are in (j,x) is $E\{V(j-1,X)\} - c$ which is seen to be independent of x. It may then be denoted by a symbol that only refers to j. Denote it by v_j, that is, let v_j be defined by

$$(4) \qquad v_j = E\{V(j-1,X)\} - c$$

Thus, v_j stands for the value to you at (j,x) of going on for at least one more period (making at least one more observation) before deciding to stop.

Now, the value to you of being in (j,x) can be written as

$$(5) \qquad V(j,x) = \max(x^+, v_j)$$

Thus, an implication of your principle for making decisions is that, when you are in (j,x), you should continue if $x^+ < v_j$ and you should stop if $x^+ > v_j$. If $x^+ = v_j$ it does not matter what you choose to do. If you follow this rule, you will in fact maximize your expected net gain, so we have arrived at the structure of an optimal decision rule.

The problem is now reduced to that of determining the sequence of numbers v_j for $j \geqq 1$. Equation (4) gives v_j in terms of $V(j-1,X)$ so by using (5) one gets

$$(6) \qquad v_j = E\{\max(X^+, v_{j-1})\} - c \qquad j > 1$$

By (6) v_j can be calculated if we know v_{j-1}, c and F, the distribution function of X. To get a starting value, consider v_1, the value to you at $(1,x)$ of making the last observation to which you are entitled before you will have to stop. Then, from (3) and (4) or directly from the assumptions of the problem, we get

$$(7) \qquad v_1 = E\{X^+\} - c$$

which can be calculated given only c and F. The other elements of the sequence are then determined by (6). However, in order to make (6) hold for $j=1$ as well, introduce the formal definition $v_0 = 0$. This definition appears reasonable by comparing (6) to the last expression in (7).

So, given c and F, the distribution function of X, the sequence of numbers v_j, $j \geqq 0$, is uniquely determined by the recursive relation

$$(8) \qquad \begin{cases} v_j = E\{\max(X^+, v_{j-1})\} - c & j \geqq 1 \\ v_0 = 0 \end{cases}$$

Now the problem has been translated into mathematics. (See Figure 1 of 4.3 for a description of the problem in the form of a decision tree.) The next step will be to wring out of *(8)* some of the information that it contains about the properties of v_j. The result of this will then be translated back into terms of the problem.

2.3 MATHEMATICAL TREATMENT

This section is devoted to a study of the properties of the sequence of real numbers v_j, $j \geqq 0$, defined by

$$(1) \qquad \begin{cases} v_j = E\{\max(X^+, v_{j-1})\} - c & j \geqq 1 \\ v_0 = 0 \end{cases}$$

which is the same as *(2.2.8)* above.

For the developments that follow (both of this model and various generalizations of it) it will prove helpful to have a concise notation for expressions like $E\{\max(X,s)\}$, where s is a real number and X a random variable with distribution function F and such that $E\{\max(X,0)\}$ is finite. Let the function T_F be defined by either one of the following (equivalent) expressions (see A1.1 and DeGroot [1970 p 246]):

$$(2a) \qquad E\{\max(X,s)\} = s + T_F(s)$$

$$(2b) \qquad T_F(s) = E\{\max(X-s,0)\}$$

$$(2c) \qquad T_F(s) = \int_s^\infty (1 - F(t))dt$$

The properties of T_F that will be used in the sequel are derived in Appendix 1.

By *(2.2.2)* and *(2a)* the expected value in *(1)* can be rewritten as

$$(3)\qquad E\{\max(X^+, v_{j-1})\} = E\{\max(X, 0, v_{j-1})\} =$$

$$= E\{\max[X, \max(v_{j-1}, 0)]\} =$$

$$= E\{\max[X, v^+_{j-1}]\} = v^+_{j-1} + T_F(v^+_{j-1})$$

so *(1)* may be rewritten as

$$(4)\qquad \begin{cases} v_j = v^+_{j-1} + T_F(v^+_{j-1}) - c & j \geqq 1 \\ v_0 = 0 \end{cases}$$

or, keeping in mind that v_0 equals zero,

$$(5)\qquad v_j = \begin{cases} T_F(0) - c & v_{j-1} \leqq 0 \\ v_{j-1} + T_F(v_{j-1}) - c & v_{j-1} > 0 \end{cases} \qquad j \geqq 1$$

Clearly $v_{j-1} \leqq 0$ implies $v_j = T_F(0) - c = v_1$ and thus, by induction

$$(6)\qquad v_1 \leqq 0 \Rightarrow v_j = v_1 \qquad j \geqq 1$$

which determines the sequence for the case $v_1 \leqq 0$. Similarly, if $v_1 > 0$ and satisfies the equation

$$(7)\qquad v_1 = v_1 + T_F(v_1) - c$$

we may again conclude (by *(5)*) that $v_j = v_1$ for $j \geqq 1$. Let us then <u>define</u> the number v by

$$(8)\qquad T_F(v) = c$$

where c is a positive constant. By *A2P1* v is uniquely determined by *(8)* and by *A2P2* $v_1 > 0$ is equivalent to $v > 0$. Hence,

$$(9)\qquad v_1 = v > 0 \Rightarrow v_j = v \qquad j \geqq 1$$

But, by *A3P3*, $v_1 > 0$ implies $v \geqq v_1$, with equality if and only if

$F(v-) = 0$ (that is, $F(t) = 0$ for all $t < v$), so

(10) $\quad (v > 0) \wedge (F(v-) = 0) \Rightarrow v_j = v_1 (=v) \qquad j \geqq 1$

This is also made plausible by Figure 1 below. Note that by *(2c)* a possible interpretation of $T_F(v)$ is the area between $y = F(t)$ and $y = 1$ and to the right of $t = v$. By *(8)* and *(4)* the notation in the figure is self-explanatory and *(10)* can be derived from it by "geometrical" means.

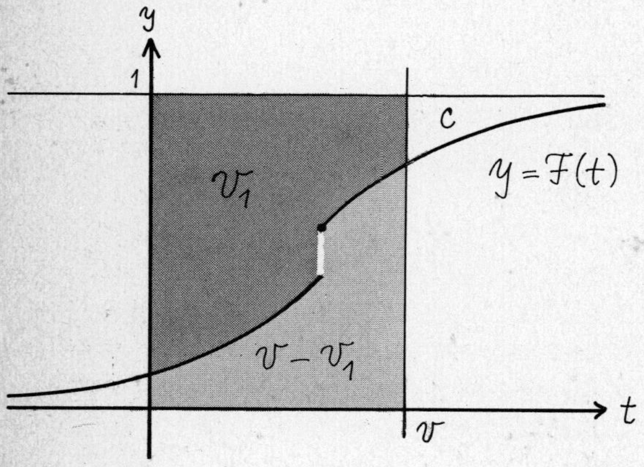

Figure 1 *v and v_1 in relation to F and c*

Now there remains the case $v > v_1 > 0$. Here $v - v_j > 0$ *(A3P4)* and $v_{j+1} - v_j > 0$ *(A3P5)* for $j \geqq 1$. Thus the sequence v_j, $j \geqq 1$, is a bounded, strictly increasing sequence of positive real number. Then it must converge, that is there exists a unique number α, such that $\alpha = \lim_{j\to\infty} v_j$ and α is positive so by *(5)* and the continuity of T_F,*(A1P5)*, it must satisfy

(11) $\quad \alpha = \alpha + T_F(\alpha) - c$

that is,

(12) $\quad T_F(\alpha) = c$

so, by *(8)* and *A2P1*, $\alpha = v$ and hence

$$(13) \qquad \lim_{j\to\infty} v_j = v$$

This amounts to the following:

$$(14) \qquad v > v_1 > 0 \Rightarrow (v > v_{j+1} > v_j,\ j \geqq 1) \wedge \lim_{j\to\infty} v_j = v$$

The left hand side of *(14)* may be reformulated as $v > 0 \wedge F(v-) \neq 0$ in analogy with *(10)* or as $v > \max(0, v_1)$ recalling that $v > 0 \Leftrightarrow v_1 > 0$ by *A2P2*.

Since in all other cases $v_j = v_1$, $j \geqq 1$, *(6)* and *(10)* may be condensed into

$$(15) \qquad v \leqq \max(0, v_1) \Rightarrow v_j = v_1 \qquad j \geqq 1$$

Obviously the left hand sides of *(14)* and *(15)* cannot both be false, nor can the right hand sides both be true, so the following equivalences hold (*A3P8*):

$$(16) \qquad v > \max(0, v_1) \Leftrightarrow (v > v_{j+1} > v_j,\ j \geqq 1) \wedge \lim_{j\to\infty} v_j = v$$

$$(17) \qquad v \leqq \max(0, v_1) \Leftrightarrow v_j = v_1 \qquad j \geqq 1$$

where v is given by *(8)*.

2.4 TRANSLATION BACK INTO THE TERMS OF THE PROBLEM

How should you choose between continuing and stopping if you want to act in such a way that your expected net gain from participating in this lottery is to be as great as possible? This is the question posed at the end of the statement of the problem in Section 2.1. We may now give an answer to it.

Recall that v_j stands for the expected value to you at (j,x) of going on for at least one more period (making at least one more observation) before stopping, c is the cost of making an observation and F summarizes all there is to know about the prize-list of the lottery and the probability of any given prize being won. It is then clear from (2.2.5) that when you are in (j,x), v_j should serve as your level of aspiration; if the value of the prize you have just won exceeds v_j, then you should stop, otherwise you should continue. Moreover, knowing c and F, you can calculate the value of v_j for any j by using (2.3.5).

This answers the question but it raises another one: How does v_j behave when j changes, or, how is your level of aspiration influenced by the number of periods that remain before you will be forced to stop? It would seem reasonable if $v_{j+1} \geqq v_j$ for all j; if you have more periods to go, then, surely, you would not lower your level of aspiration. This is in fact the case, which is shown in the previous section. However, by (2.3.16) and (2.3.17) more precise results are available, namely necessary and sufficient conditions under which $v_{j+1} > v_j$ and $v_j = v_1$ for all $j \geqq 1$, respectively. We shall now interpret these results and see whether they make sense from an economic point of view.

Let us start by interpreting the number v, defined by $T_F(v) = c$, that is, $E\{\max(X-v,0)\} = c$ (see (2.3.8) and (2.3.2b)), or

$$(1) \qquad E\{(X-v)^+\} - c = 0$$

Your net gain from buying just one ticket and then quitting is $X^+ - c$, the expected value of which is denoted by v_1, that is,

$$(2) \qquad v_1 = E\{X^+\} - c$$

On comparing these two expressions, we find that v is the amount by which the value of each prize of the lottery must be reduced for v_1 to become zero; to reduce by v means to add $-v$. Clearly v and v_1 must have the same sign, and when one of them is zero, then so is the other (A2P2). They may also be regarded as measures of the favourability of the lottery, that is, measures of the balance between F and c.

To get a more precise idea of what they measure, let us see how their values will change if the balance between F and c is changed. Firstly, suppose the cost of a ticket is changed by Δc while F remains the same. Then $E\{X^+\}$ is unchanged, so, by *(2)*, v_1 changes by $-\Delta c$, since $v_1 + c$ is to remain constant (see Figure 2.3.1). (By *(1)*, v will change as well and in the same direction as v_1). Secondly, let c remain constant while an amount h is added to the value of each prize (the curve $y = F(t)$ is shifted h units to the right). Then, by *(1)*, v will change by h units, since $E\{(X-v)^+\}$ is to remain constant (v_1 will change in the same direction, by *(2)*). Hence, a change in the cost of a ticket bears a simple relation to the corresponding change in v_1 whereas a change in the values of the prizes (adding the same amount to each) bears an equally simple relation to the corresponding change in v.

Consider a favourable lottery, one for which $v > 0$ and $v_1 > 0$. Suppose further that the lottery is such that the value of its least valuable prize is actually v (or more). Since there is a prize for each ticket, you are then certain to win v (at the least), that is, $F(v-) = 0$. By *(1)* and *(2)* (see also Figure 2.3.1) we find that $v_1 = v + E\{(X-v)^+\} - c = v$ for such a lottery, and hence $v_j = v_1$ for $j \geqq 1$, by *(2.3.9)*. Thus, your optimal level of aspiration is positive and never changes. You should buy one ticket, which will give you at least v with certainty, and then quit, no matter how many tickets you are allowed to buy. (By *(1)*, the expected improvement of your net gain will be zero if you continue.) Note that your <u>expected</u> net gain from following this procedure will be v, which is positive. However, if you are unlucky you will only win the least valuable prize so that your <u>actual</u> net gain will be $v - c$ which may be negative. What makes this case interesting is not that it should be a particularly favourable one but that it is a case where your level of aspiration should be uninfluenced by the number of tickets you are allowed to buy.

Suppose instead that the lottery is such that the value of its least valuable prize is less than v, that is, $F(v-) > 0$. Then $v > v_1 > 0$, and we have, by *(2.3.14)*, $v > v_{j+1} > v_j$ for $j \geqq 1$, and $\lim_{j\to\infty} v_j = v$. This means that you should lower your level of aspiration as you approach the point of forced stopping. When you have fewer observations left, you should be content with a less valuable prize than before, or, stated the other way around, the more observations at your disposal, the more demanding you should be. Moreover, there is a finite limit to your being demanding; no matter how far away you are from the point of forced stopping, your level of aspiration should not exceed v. It may be arbitrarily close to it, however, so v may be regarded as your optimal level of aspiration in case you will never be forced to stop.

Consider now a non-favourable lottery, one for which $v \leqq 0$ or $v_1 \leqq 0$. We found above that v and v_1 always have the same sign, so here they are either both of them zero or both of them negative. In either case, it follows from *(2.3.6)* that $v_j = v_1$, $j \geqq 1$, for such a lottery. This may be seen by the following argument.

Clearly, if $v_j < 0$ for some $j \geqq 1$, you should not continue the process beyond state (j,x) whatever x is. Your situation one period earlier, when you have $j + 1$ instead of j more lottery tickets at your disposal, is then just the same as that when you may only buy one more ticket; you <u>know</u> that the best thing for you to do is to buy <u>at the most</u> one more ticket although you may not be forced to stop after having bought it. Thus, $v_{j+1} = v_1$. Now, $v_1 < 0$, so this is true for <u>any</u> state, since $v_1 < 0$ implies $v_2 = v_1 \leqq 0$ and so on (by mathematical induction). Thus you should never buy even the "one more" lottery ticket, that is, you should refuse to participate in the lottery, for your expected net gain from continuing is always negative. Let us call such a lottery <u>unfair</u>.

By a similar argument, $v_1 = 0$ is seen to imply $v_j = v_1 = 0$ for $j \geqq 1$, that is, your expected net gain from continuing is always zero. However, this value is achieved by several decision rules. You may refuse to participate, you may continue until you have won a prize having a positive value, or you may stop any time before that. Essentially, you should be indifferent to participating in this kind of a lottery. Let us call such a lottery _fair_.

Since this exhausts all possibilities, we may partition the set of conceivable lotteries by classifying each lottery according to the sign of v (or that of v_1). Thus, we call a lottery _favourable_ if $v > 0$, _fair_ if $v = 0$, and _unfair_ if $v < 0$. It follows from the above that you should refuse to participate in an unfair lottery, accept to participate in a favourable one, and be indifferent to participating in a fair one.

We may also classify lotteries according to how your levels of aspiration should vary with the number of tickets that you may buy. Thus, the set of lotteries for which your level of aspiration should be the higher the more lottery tickets you may buy includes all lotteries for which $v > v_1 > 0$ and nothing more. Note that this is exactly what _(2.3.16)_ expresses. Also, each such lottery is favourable.

Similarly, all other lotteries are such that your level of aspiration should be the same, no matter for how long you may continue. This is what _(2.3.17)_ expresses. Moreover, such a lottery is favourable if and only if $v = v_1 > 0$.

These results are summarized in Table 1:

$$
\begin{array}{ll}
\text{unfair} & \left\{ \; v < 0 \right. \\[2ex]
\text{fair} & \left\{ \; v = 0 \right. \\[2ex]
\text{favourable} & \left\{ \begin{array}{l} (v > 0) \wedge (v = v_1) \\[1ex] (v > 0) \wedge (v \neq v_1) \end{array} \right.
\end{array}
$$

$$
\left. \begin{array}{l} v_j = v_1, \quad j \geq 1 \\[3ex] (v > v_{j+1} > v_j, \; j \geq 1) \wedge \\[1ex] \wedge \lim_{j \to \infty} v_j = v \end{array} \right.
$$

Table 1   How to classify a lottery (see the text).

For a favourable or a fair lottery, v may be interpreted as your optimal level of aspiration if you will never be forced to stop (this will be proved in Chapter 3). However, for an unfair lottery this interpretation must be given to v_1. Thus, an unfair lottery is one in which you should not participate, no matter for how long you may continue. But those are the lotteries for which v_1 is negative. Hence, if a lottery is such that you should not participate in it if you may buy only one ticket, then it is an unfair lottery so you should not participate even if you may buy an unlimited number of tickets. Please note this conclusion.

Also note that "favourable" etc. is meant from your point of view and on an assumption of "expected net gain" being consistent with your expected utility. However, in the end you may very well regret ever having started buying tickets (even if the lottery is a favourable one) although at each decision point it seemed more advantageous to continue than to stop.

Suppose you decide to participate in a favourable lottery for which $v > v_1 > 0$. You start in $(j,0)$ for some $j > k > 1$, and you follow an optimal decision rule all the time. Suppose you are then led to turning down the first $k - 1$ prizes but to accepting the k:th one. Thus, you decide to stop when you are in state $(j-k, x)$, where $x > v_{j-k}$, and you have then spent kc on the lottery tickets. You may then regret ever having started, since you have no guarantee that $x > kc$. However, no one can blame you for having made wrong decisions at any point during the process, since at any previous point the prospects seemed to warrant the extra outlay for going on. At each point it is only the extra outlay that should count; what you have already spent is gone irrevocably.

2.5 THE SOLUTION

We have now answered the question posed at the end of the introduction to this chapter. If you know the construction of the lottery, the cost of a ticket and the number of tickets you may buy, you will now be able to act so as to maximize your expected net gain from participating in the lottery. In order to achieve this you should follow a decision rule of the form

(1) If you are in (j,x), $j \geqq 1$, then <u>stop</u> if $x^+ > v_j$; <u>continue</u> if $x^+ < v_j$

where (j,x) denotes the state in which you are: There are no more than j tickets to be bought before you will be forced to stop, and the prize for your latest ticket has the value x. The number v_j which serves as your level of aspiration, may be calculated (recursively) for any value of j by use of *(2.3.5)* given only the construction of the lottery and the cost of a ticket.

Thus, your level of aspiration should depend only on the number of tickets that remain before you are forced to stop. Moreover, in some lotteries you should buy at the most one ticket before stopping (see 2.4). We disregard such lotteries from further consideration since they do not give rise to any sequential decision-making problem. In all other lotteries, your level of aspiration should be the higher the further away you are from the point of forced stopping. However, even if you may continue for ever, your level of aspiration is a well-defined finite number, v, which is the limit to which v_j tends as j increases. Thus, in a process with no forced stopping, your level of aspiration should always be the same, no matter how many tickets you have bought. (The existence of an optimal decision rule for such a process is proved in Section 3.7.)

The following conclusions may be worth noting:

- You should participate (buy at least one ticket) in a lottery of this kind if and <u>only if</u> it is favourable to participate on a one-period basis, i.e. on the condition that you may only buy <u>one</u> ticket (see 2.4).
- At each decision point the expected value of continuing is independent of the value of stopping (v_j is independent of x).

Clearly this is unlike most development work, for example (just to take one of the examples of 1.1), where a project may seem unfavourable if quick results are required, whereas the same project may be regarded as very promising if the dead-line for results is set at some more distant date. Also, results can usually be saved, the work of later periods being attempts to improve earlier results; the prospects of continuing will then depend on the value of the available results (a good result may be harder to improve than a bad).

It will be interesting to modify the process in such a way that these features disappear. Both of them seem to be at least partly accounted for by the rule that says that old prizes are foregone upon continuation of the process; like a roulette-wheel the process has no memory, and since you have to "give back" old prizes before continuing, you start from zero in each period. All results are quick results in the sense that what you collect upon stopping is the prize for your latest ticket.

A possible modification would then be to change the rules in such a way that what you collect upon stopping is any one of the prizes for your previous tickets. Then the process will have a memory, and what you eventually collect will no more necessarily be the prize for your latest ticket. Or will it? The next chapter is devoted to a study of the consequences of making this modification.

3 The Basic Model with Recall

3.1 INTRODUCTION

In the problem described in the previous chapter you were not allowed to carry over results from one period to the next; if you decided to go on, the prize to which your latest ticket gave you a right would be gone irrevocably. You had to start from scratch for each new ticket in the sense that previous prizes were all intentionally foregone by you; they might as well be regarded as forgotten for ever. Thus, present decisions should never be influenced by past results.

This assumption will now be dropped. When you stop, you may instead collect the prize for any one of your previous tickets. If you decide to go on, you then still have the option of collecting the prize for your latest ticket at some future point. Thus, present decisions may be influenced by past results, since the latter may be recalled at any later point. The question to be answered is still primarily that of determining how you should choose between continuing and stopping if you want to act so as to maximize your expected net gain.

The way of finding a precise answer will be similar to the one followed in Chapter 2 and the properties of the two models will be compared in various respects. Furthermore, we attempt to give more "conversational" arguments for some of the results obtained by mathematical means. We also treat the question whether an optimal decision rule exists. This has simply been assumed to be the case so far. Finally, we introduce the concept of a myopic decision rule and examine whether such a rule may be an optimal decision rule.

3.2 THE PROBLEM

You are invited to participate in a lottery, the construction of which is completely known (see 2.1). When you buy a ticket, it is drawn at random from among all the lottery tickets. You will then know which prize it will win you and the value of this prize.

At each such point you must decide whether you want to stop or to continue buying lottery tickets. If you stop, you now have the option of either leaving without collecting a prize or collecting the prize for any one of your previous tickets. If you continue, you refrain from collecting a prize at this point, but you now keep the possibility of collecting the prize for any previous ticket at some point in the future.

As before, you may stop whenever you like, but once you have stopped you may not buy any more tickets. You will also eventually be forced to stop, for you may buy at the most a given finite number of lottery tickets.

The following concepts are taken over from the previous model (see 2.1): Your net gain from participating in the lottery is taken to be the value of what you collect upon stopping minus the cost of the tickets you have bought. At any time, the value to you of continuing or stopping is taken to be your expected net gain from choosing the respective alternative.

How should you choose between continuing and stopping if you want to act so as to maximize your expected net gain from participating in the lottery?

This is the problem to be solved. We shall also see what happens if you may continue indefinitely, that is, if there is no bound to the number of tickets that you may buy.

3.3 TRANSLATION INTO MATHEMATICS

Since not very much is changed from the basic model, many concepts, the arguments that led to their consideration and much of the notation may be taken over more or less literally from Section 2.2.

Thus, the process is still equivalent to one of observing sequentially a random variable having a given distribution function, the random variable being the value of the prize for a ticket drawn at random from among all the lottery tickets. The distribution function of this random variable is given to you from your knowledge of the construction of the lottery. Moreover, successive drawings may be regarded as independent observations of the same random variable since before drawing a new ticket, you must always put back your old one among the other tickets. Let the random variable be denoted by Y and its distribution function by F.

Your situation or the <u>state of the process</u> may still be exhaustively characterized by an ordered pair (j,x), where j denotes the number of tickets you may still buy before you will be forced to stop and x stands for the value to you of the prize that you will collect if you stop at once. What is new here is that when you stop, you may choose to collect the prize of <u>any one</u> of your earlier tickets, not just that of the latest one. Since you want to get as much as possible out of the process, x will be the value to you of the most valuable one of the prizes for your earlier tickets.

You always start in $(n,0)$ for some integer $n \geq 1$, that is you may buy at most n tickets and so far the value of the prize you may collect is neither positive nor negative. Agree to call it a "prize" anyway. Then the condition that you may leave without a prize when you stop is incorporated in the rule above. You collect the most valuable one of the prizes from among your previous tickets. The very least you will get is zero.

If you stop at (j,x), the state of the process is changed into $(0,x)$ and you collect x^+. If you continue, you pay c and let the state of the process be changed into $(j-1, \max(Y,x))$, where

$$\text{(1)} \qquad \max(Y,x) = \begin{cases} Y & x < Y \\ x & x \geqq Y \end{cases}$$

This is so because according to the new conditions, when you continue, you do not lose the option of collecting the prize for an earlier ticket; you will always be able to collect at least x. However, if your new ticket wins you a prize the value of which (Y) is greater than the prize value of any of the earlier tickets (x), then this is what you will collect if your next decision is to stop. Note that Y is a random variable, the value of which will be unknown to you until the new ticket has been drawn. Thus, if you continue, you do not know which state will be the next, only that the number of possible remaining observations will have decreased by one and that the value of what you may then collect will <u>not</u> have decreased.

Suppose that the state of the process is (j,x), $j \geqq 1$, and that you are about to decide whether you are going to stop or continue. You want to choose the alternative that has the greatest value to you (expected net gain) and you want to stick to this principle in every subsequent decision regarding the process that you may have to make. Let $V(j,x)$ denote the value to you of engaging yourself in the process on these conditions. Then

$$V(j,x) = \max \left\{ \begin{array}{l} \text{the value to you of stopping at } (j,x) \\ \text{the value to you of being in } (j-1, \max(Y,x)) \text{ minus } c \end{array} \right\}$$

But since "value to you" is still taken to be expected net gain and since "stopping at (j,x)" means "being in $(0,x)$", the value to you of being in (j,x) can be expressed as follows:

$$(2) \qquad V(j,x) = \max\left\{\begin{array}{l} V(0,x) \\ E\{V(j-1, \max(Y,x))\} - c \end{array}\right\}$$

No confusion should arise from using "$V(j,x)$" again, since it will be clear from the context to which case it refers.

The value to you of stopping at (j,x) is then equal to $V(0,x)$. From what was said above it is clear that you will never accept a prize of negative value to you. As before this is made apparent from the notation, by letting the value of what you collect on stopping at (j,x) be denoted by x^+ (see (2.2.2)). Thus,

$$(3) \qquad V(0,x) = x^+ = \begin{cases} 0 & x \leqq 0 \\ x & x > 0 \end{cases}$$

The value to you of continuing when you are in (j,x) is $E\{V(j-1, \max(Y,x))\} - c$. It is no longer independent of x, so it will have to be denoted by a symbol that refers to x as well as to j. Denote it by $v_j(x)$, that is let $v_j(x)$ be defined by

$$(4) \qquad v_j(x) = E\{V(j-1, \max(Y,x))\} - c$$

Then $v_j(x)$ stands for the value to you at (j,x) of continuing for at least one more period (making at least one more observation) before deciding to stop.

Now the value to you of being in (j,x) can be written as

$$(5) \qquad V(j,x) = \max(x^+, v_j(x))$$

so the structure of the solution of the problem remains the same as before: When in (j,x), you go on if $x^+ < v_j(x)$ and you stop if $x^+ > v_j(x)$; if $x^+ = v_j(x)$ it does not matter what you choose to do. However, here your levels of aspiration may vary with x.

The problem is now reduced to that of determining the sequence of functions v_j for $j \geqq 1$. By (4) and (5) one gets

$$(6) \qquad v_j(x) = E\{\max[\max(Y,x)^+, v_{j-1}(\max(Y,x))]\} - c \qquad j > 1$$

by which $v_j(x)$ can be determined recursively. A starting condition is obtained by setting $j = 1$ in (4) and using (3). Then $v_1(x)$ can be written as

$$(7) \qquad v_1(x) = E\{V(0, \max(Y,x))\} - c = E\{\max(Y,x^+)\} - c$$

which can be calculated given only c and F. The other elements of the sequence are then determined by (6). In order to make (6) hold for $j = 1$ as well, introduce the formal definition $v_0(x) = x^+$. This is a reasonable definition since by formally setting $j = 1$ in (6) and using it, one gets (7). However, $v_0(x)$ is not to be given an interpretation such as that of $v_j(x)$ for $j \geqq 1$.

Thus, given c and F, the distribution function of Y, the sequence of functions v_j, $j \geqq 0$, is uniquely determined by the recursive relation

$$(8) \qquad \begin{cases} v_j(x) = E\{\max[v_0(\max(y,x)), v_{j-1}(\max(Y,x))]\} - c & j \geqq 1 \\ v_0(x) = x^+ \end{cases}$$

Now the problem has been translated into mathematics. (See Figure 1 of 4.4 for a description of the problem in the form of a decision tree.) The next step will be to study the properties of $v_j(x)$ and if possible to derive an explicit expression for it, that is, one that does not contain any other element of the sequence of functions but only c, F, j, and x.

3.4 MATHEMATICAL TREATMENT

This section is devoted to a study of the sequence of functions $v_j(x)$, $x \in R$, $j \geqq 0$, defined recursively by

$$(1)\qquad \begin{cases} v_j(x) = E\{\max[v_0(\max(Y,x)),\ v_{j-1}(\max(Y,x))]\} - c \\ v_0(x) = x^+ \end{cases}$$

which is the same as *(3.3.8)* above. The aim is to find an explicit expression for $v_j(x)$, where j ranges over the set of positive integers and x over the set of real numbers. By "explicit expression" is meant one which (unlike *(1)*) does not refer to any other element of the sequence of functions but only to the basic entities j, x, c, and F. In order to get an idea of the structure of the general expression, $v_j(x)$ will first be derived explicitly for $j=1$, 2 3. Then the argument proceeds by induction.

First note that $v_0(\max(Y,x)) = \max(Y,x,0) = \max(Y,x^+)$ so that for $j = 1$ we have, by *(1)*,

$$(2)\qquad v_1(x) = E\{\max(Y,x^+)\} - c = x^+ + T_F(x^+) - c$$

where the last equality follows from *A1P1*. Moreover, for $j \geqq 0$ we may rewrite *(1)* as

$$(3)\qquad v_{j+1}(x) = E\{\max[0,\ v_j(\max(Y,x)) - v_0(\max(Y,x))]\} + \\ + E\{\max(Y,x^+)\} - c$$

from which is seen that $v_j(\cdot) - v_0(\cdot)$ will be a recurrent expression in the sequel. Introduce the abbreviation

$$(4)\qquad w_j(x) = v_j(x) - v_0(x)$$

Then, since $v_0(x) = x^+$, by *(2)*, *(4)*, and *(3)*, *(1)* may be written as

$$(5)\qquad \begin{cases} w_{j+1}(x) = E\{\max[0,\ w_j(\max(Y,x))]\} + T_F(x^+) - c \qquad j \geqq 1 \\ w_1(x) = T_F(x^+) - c \end{cases}$$

Recall that v is uniquely defined by $T_F(v) = c$ (see *A2P1*). Then, by

A1P4, $T_F(t) - c$ is non-negative if and only if $t \leqq v$. Thus $w_1(x) \geqq 0$ if and only if $x^+ \leqq v$. Set $j = 1$ in *(5)* to get

$$(6) \qquad w_2(x) = \int_R \max[0, w_1(t,x^+)]dF(t) + T_F(x^+) - c =$$

$$= \int_R \max[0, T_F(\max(t,x^+)) - c]dF(t) + T_F(x^+) - c$$

The integral in the last expression vanishes for $x^+ > v$ and then $w_2(x) = w_1(x)$. Clearly, $w_j(x) \leqq 0$ implies $w_{j+1}(x) = T_F(x^+) - c = w_1(x)$ by *(5)*. Since $w_1(x) < 0$ for $x^+ > v$ it follows by induction that $w_j(x) = w_1(x)$, $j \geqq 1$, for $x^+ > v$.

In the remaining case, $x^+ \leqq v$, the relevant domain of integration becomes $\{t|\max(t,x^+) \leqq v\} = \{t|t \leqq v \wedge x^+ \leqq v\}$ which is the union of the two disjoint sets $\{t|t \leqq x^+\}$ and $\{t|x^+ < t \leqq v\}$. The integral in *(6)* can then be written as

$$(7) \qquad \int_{-\infty}^{x^+} [T_F(x^+) - c]dF(t) + \int_{x^+}^{v} [T_F(t) - c]dF(t)$$

which can be reduced to

$$(8) \qquad T_F(x^+)F(x^+) - cF(v) + \int_{x^+}^{v} T_F(t)dF(t)$$

By *A1P11* the integral in *(8)* can be developed into

$$(9) \qquad T_{F^2}(x^+) - T_F(x^+)F(x^+) - T_F(x^+) - [T_{F^2}(v) - T_F(v)F(v) - T_F(v)]$$

Now it is time to put things together again. Use $c = T_F(v)$ and substitute *(9)* for the integral in *(8)*. Then *(8)* becomes

$$(10) \qquad T_{F^2}(x^+) - T_F(x^+) - T_{F^2}(v) + c$$

Finally, substitute *(10)* for the integral in *(6)* to get

$$(11) \qquad w_2(x) = T_{F^2}(x^+) - T_{F^2}(v) \qquad x^+ \leqq v$$

By an entirely analogous argument, starting from *(11)* and *(5)*, one finds

$$(12) \qquad w_3(x) = T_{F^3}(x^+) - T_{F^3}(v) \qquad x^+ \leqq v$$

It seems reasonable to try to prove that $w_j(x) = T_{F^j}(x^+) - T_{F^j}(v)$ is the general expression for $w_j(x)$, $x^+ \leqq v$. We try a proof by induction. Thus, assume that

$$(13) \qquad w_j(x) = T_{F^j}(x^+) - T_{F^j}(v), \; x^+ \leqq v \qquad \text{for some } j \geqq 1$$

and insert *(13)* in *(5)* to get

$$(14) \qquad w_{j+1}(x) - w_1(x) = E\{\max[0, T_{F^j}(\max(Y, x^+)) - T_{F^j}(v)]\} =$$

$$= \int_D [T_{F^j}(\max(t, x^+)) - T_{F^j}(v)]dF(t)$$

where $D = \{t \mid \max(t, x^+) \leqq v\} = \{t \mid t \leqq x^+\} \cup \{t \mid x^+ < t \leqq v\}$.

Then the integral in *(14)* becomes

$$(15) \qquad \int_{-\infty}^{x^+} [T_{F^j}(x^+) - T_{F^j}(v)]dF(t) + \int_{x^+}^{v} [T_{F^j}(t) - T_{F^j}(v)]dF(t) =$$

$$= T_{F^j}(x^+)F(x^+) - T_{F^j}(v)F(v) + \int_{x^+}^{v} T_{F^j}(t)dF(t)$$

which by *A1P11* can be reduced to

$$(16) \qquad T_{F^{j+1}}(x^+) - T_F(x^+) - T_{F^{j+1}}(v) + T_F(v)$$

so that *(14)* becomes (recall that $w_1(x) = T_F(x^+) - T_F(v)$)

$$(17) \qquad w_{j+1}(x) = T_{F^{j+1}}(x^+) - T_{F^{j+1}}(v) \qquad x^+ \leqq v$$

Thus, if *(13)* is true for some j, it is also true for $j + 1$. It is true for $j = 1$, however, so by induction it must be true for every $j \geqq 1$.

Then

$$(18)\qquad w_j(x) = \begin{cases} T_{F^j}(x^+) - T_{F^j}(v) & x^+ \leqq v \\ T_F(x^+) - T_F(v) & x^+ > v \end{cases} \qquad j \geqq 1$$

By the monotonocity of T_F (see *A1P4*) it is clear that $w_j(x)$ always has the same sign as $v - x^+$.

In terms of $v_j(x)$ these results can be expressed as (see *(4)*)

$$(19)\qquad \begin{cases} v_j(x) = \begin{cases} x^+ + T_{F^j}(x^+) - T_{F^j}(v) & x^+ \leqq v \\ x^+ + T_F(x^+) - T_F(v) & x^+ > v \end{cases} \qquad j \geqq 1 \\ v_0(x) = x^+ \end{cases}$$

and

$$(20)\qquad v_j(x) \begin{smallmatrix} \geqq \\ < \end{smallmatrix} v_0(x) \Longleftrightarrow x^+ \begin{smallmatrix} \leqq \\ > \end{smallmatrix} v \qquad j \geqq 1$$

where the signs on the same level belong together.

Only for $x^+ \leqq v$ does $v_j(x)$ vary with j. Then, by *(19)* and the definition of T_F (see *A1D1*) $v_j(x)$ can be written as

$$(21)\qquad v_j(x) = x^+ + \int_{x^+}^{v} (1 - F^j(t))dt = v - \int_{x^+}^{v} F^j(t)dt$$

where the last integral obeys the inequalities $0 \leqq \int_{x^+}^{v} F^j(t)dt \leqq vF^j(v)$. But $F^j(v) \leqq F(v) < 1$ by *A1P4*, so the integral tends to zero uniformly in x as j increases. Thus,

$$(22)\qquad \lim_{j\to\infty} v_j(x) = v \qquad x^+ \leqq v$$

Moreover, by *(21)*

$$(23) \qquad v - v_j(x) \geqq 0 \qquad x^+ \leqq v$$

and

$$(24) \qquad v_{j+1}(x) - v_j(x) = \int_{x^+}^{v} F^j(t)(1 - F(t))dt \geqq 0 \qquad x^+ \leqq v$$

where strict inequality holds in both expressions if and only if $x^+ < v$ and $F(v-) > 0$.

Since T_F is continuous (*A1P5*) and has a right-hand derivative everywhere (*A1P8*), it is clear from *(19)* that these properties are possessed by $v_j(x)$ as well. Moreover, by *A1P8* we get for $j \geqq 1$

$$(25) \qquad v < 0 \Rightarrow v_j'(x+0) = \begin{cases} 0 & x < 0 \\ F(x) & x \geqq 0 \end{cases}$$

$$(26) \qquad v \geqq 0 \Rightarrow v_j'(x+0) = \begin{cases} 0 & x < 0 \\ F^j(x) & 0 \leqq x < v \\ F(x) & v \leqq x \end{cases}$$

Let a be a number (possibly $-\infty$) such that $F(t) = 0$ for $t < a$ and $F(t) > 0$ for $t > a$, that is, $a = \sup\{t|F(t) = 0\}$. By *(25)* and *(26)*, $v_j(x)$ is then seen to be constant for $x < a^+$ and strictly increasing for $x \geqq a^+$.

These conclusions are illustrated in Figure 1 for the case where $x^+ < v$ and $F(v-) \neq 0$. Recall that $F(v) < 1$. Hence, $0 < F(v-) \leqq F(v) < 1$ in this case which implies $0 < F^j(v-) \leqq F(v-) < 1$ for any $j \geqq 1$.

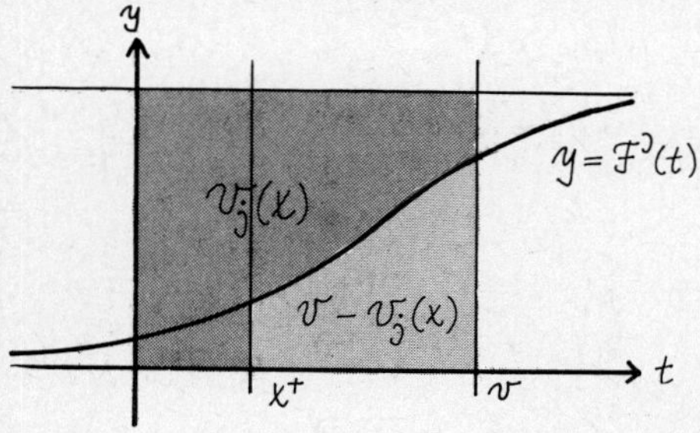

Figure 1 *v and $v_j(x)$ in relation to F^j*

By *(21)*, $v - v_j(x)$ corresponds to the area between $t = x^+$ and $t = v$ that is above the horizontal axis and below the curve $y = F^j(t)$. The area of the rest of the rectangle bounded by the axes and the lines $y = 1$ and $t = v$ corresponds to $v_j(x)$. Note that $F^{j+1}(t) < F^j(t)$ at least for some open interval containing v (A1.3). Then *(24)*, *(23)*, and *(22)* are seen to hold from the figure. (Cf Figure 1 of Section 2.3.)

To see the similarity between this model and that of the previous chapter, note that by *(21)* the condition $(x^+ < v) \wedge (F(v-) \neq 0)$ is equivalent to $v > \max(x^+, v_1(x))$; for a proof, see *A4P5*. This is also seen from the figure. Thus, for $j \geqq 0$

$$(27) \qquad v > \max(x^+, v_1(x)) \Rightarrow v > v_{j+1}(x) > v_j(x) \wedge \lim_{j\to\infty} v_j(x) = v$$

Then the opposite condition, that is, $(x^+ \geqq v) \vee (F(v-) = 0)$, is equivalent to $v \leqq \max(x^+, v_1(x))$. Thus, by *(19)*, *(20)* and *(24)*

$$(28) \qquad v \leqq \max(x^+, v_1(x)) \Rightarrow v_j(x) = v_1(x) \qquad j \geqq 1$$

Obviously the left hand sides of *(27)* and *(28)* cannot both be false, nor can the right hand sides both be true, so both implications work "backwards" as well and the following equivalences hold for all $j \geqq 1$ (*(29)* for $j = 0$ as well):

$$(29) \qquad v > \max(x^+, v_1(x)) \Leftrightarrow v > v_{j+1}(x) > v_j(x) \wedge \lim_{j\to\infty} v_j(x) = v$$

$$(30) \qquad v \leqq \max(x^+, v_1(x)) \Leftrightarrow v_j(x) = v_1(x)$$

Do not hesitate to compare them to *(2.3.16)* and *(2.3.17)*.

3.5 TRANSLATION BACK INTO THE TERMS OF THE PROBLEM

3.5.1 The optimal decision rule. The central result of the previous section is that the equation *(3.3.8)* which says

$$(1)\qquad \begin{cases} v_j(x) = E\{\max[v_0(\max(Y,x)),\ v_{j-1}(\max(Y,x))]\} - c & j \geqq 1 \\ v_0(x) = x^+ \end{cases}$$

has the unique solution (see *(3.4.19)*)

$$(2)\qquad \begin{cases} v_j(x) = \begin{cases} x^+ + T_{F^j}(x^+) - T_{F^j}(v) & x^+ \leqq v \\ x^+ + T_F(x^+) - T_F(v) & x^+ > v \end{cases} & j \geqq 1 \\ v_0(x) = x^+ \end{cases}$$

where v is defined as before by $T_F(v) = c$ (see *A2D1* and *A2P1*).

In Section 3.3 the number $v_j(x)$ was defined to be the value to you of continuing for at least one more period before stopping, provided that you are in state (j,x). Similarly, $v_0(x) = x^+$ stands for the value of stopping at (j,x), that is, of going straight to state $(0,x)$ which puts an end to the process. By *(2)*, $v_j(x)$ can be calculated for any state, since F and c (and hence v) are known. Then, by *(3.3.5)*, in order to behave so as to maximize your expected net gain, you should choose between stopping and continuing according to the following rule:

(2a) If you are in (j,x), then stop, if $x^+ > v_j(x)$; continue, if $x^+ < v_j(x)$

If (j,x) is such that $x^+ = v_j(x)$ it does not matter what you choose to do. $v_j(x)$ is then your optimal level of aspiration when you are in (j,x), corresponding to v_j of a process without recall.

We shall now study some of the implications of *(2)* and *(2a)* and compare them to the corresponding results of Chapter 2 regarding a process without recall.

3.5.2 Properties of monotonicity in j. Your optimal level of aspiration will now depend on x^+, the value of what you may collect upon stopping. However, by *(5.4.29)* and *(5.4.30)*, for any fixed x, $v_j(x)$ as a function of j is seen to have the same properties of monotonocity as the sequence of numbers v_j (see *(2.3.16)* and *(2.3.17)*). In fact, substituting $v_0(x)$ for x^+ in *(5.4.29)* and *(5.4.30)*, we get

$$(3) \qquad v > \max(v_0(x), v_1(x)) \Leftrightarrow (v > v_{j+1}(x) > v_j(x),\ j \geqq 1) \wedge \wedge \lim_{j\to\infty} v_j(x) = v$$

$$(4) \qquad v \leqq \max(v_0(x), v_1(x)) \Leftrightarrow v_j(x) = v_1(x),\ j \geqq 1$$

and by just dropping "(x)" everywhere in *(3)* and *(4)* we get *(2.3.16)* and *(2.3.17)*. Then, for any fixed x, most of what was said about v_j in Section 2.3 holds true for $v_j(x)$ as well.

This may also be seen by the following argument. If x remains fixed while j changes, you are not making any progress in the intervening periods. You pass up all intervening observations, that is, you behave as if you were making these observations without recall, actually without even looking at them. Then at least the direction of change of your optimal level of aspiration should be the same as if these observations had been make without recall.

Such a situation will occur if, for example, your resources unexpectedly diminish so that you will be forced to stop earlier than you had thought originally. Then you find yourself in, say, state (j,x) instead of $(j + k,\ x)$ and you should adjust your level of aspiration accordingly. However, your optimal level of aspiration should only depend on the possible number of remaining observations and on the value of the largest observation made so far, the latter of which is still x. Then all you need to know for adjusting your level of aspiration is the state you are in, in this case (j,x), not how you got there. Since x is unchanged, your adjusted level of aspiration should be the same as if you had actually made k observations without recall, starting from $(j + k, x)$. Seeing this as part of a corresponding process without recall seems to imply that the direction of the adjustment of the level of aspiration for a similar change of states should be the same, whether the underlying process is one with recall or not.

However, for a process with recall, the actual values, both of the levels of aspiration in the two states and of their difference (unless zero), will in general be different from those of a process without recall: In the case in question, you always have recall to x^+ and all your future observations will be made with recall; when taken together this will in general constitute an advantage to you as compared to the corresponding case without recall.

There are some clear exceptions to this. Recall will certainly be of no value to you if you will never conceivably use it. A trivial case is when you are in state $(0,x)$. Then you just stop and collect x^+. There is nothing to recall since you may not continue. A somewhat less trivial case occurs when you are in state $(1,0)$. You are then forced to stop after having made the next observation. However, you will collect at least zero whether you stop right away or make the last observation, so you are in no way better off if you may make the last observation with recall than if you may only make it without recall. Your expected net gain from continuing will then be the same in the two cases. This is confirmed by (2) and (2.3.4), the expression for $v_1(0)$ being equal to that of v_1.

A third very much less trivial example is suggested by the mathematical treatment of the models. It follows from (3) and (4) that $\lim_{j\to\infty} v_j(x) = v$ if $v \geqq 0$, where v is defined by $T_F(v) = c$. Moreover, for the corresponding process without recall, it follows from (2.3.16) and *(2.3.17)* that $\lim_{j\to\infty} v_j = v$ if $v \geqq 0$, where v is the same number as above (see *A2P1*). Thus, if you enter a promising process with no limit to the number of observations that you may make, then your expected net gain from participating will be the same, whether you make observations with or without recall. In both cases you should go on making observations until you have made one the value of which exceeds a certain constant. Moreover, the same constant will be used in the two cases, for you will then never use the possibility of recalling an earlier observation even if you may do so. Hence you should always behave as if you were participating in the corresponding process without recall, that is, the same constant level of aspiration should be used in the two cases.

3.5.3 Another way of formulating the optimal decision rule. So far there does not seem to be any fundamental difference between observing without recall and observing with recall, apart from the optimal levels of aspiration depending on x in the latter case if you may only make a finite number of observations. However, in order to apply the optimal decision rule *(2a)*, all you need to know when you are in (j,x) is whether x^+ is greater than or less than $v_j(x)$. But by *(3.4.20)* (or straight from *(2)*, remembering the monotonicity of T_F) the following equivalence holds for all values of x:

$$(5) \qquad x^+ \begin{smallmatrix}<\\=\\>\end{smallmatrix} v_j(x) \iff x^+ \begin{smallmatrix}<\\=\\>\end{smallmatrix} v \qquad j \geqq 1$$

Thus, you may just as well follow the rule

$$(5a) \qquad \text{If you are in } (j,x)\text{, then} \quad \begin{matrix}\underline{\text{stop}} & \text{if } x^+ > v \\ \underline{\text{continue}} & \text{if } x^+ < v\end{matrix} \qquad j \geqq 1$$

You are indifferent to the two alternatives if $x^+ = v$. It is still the same old v, uniquely defined by the equation $T_F(v) = c$.

It follows from *(5)* that the rule given by *(2a)* is equivalent to the one stated above. They are just two different ways of expressing the same thing. However, the latter is more convenient to apply, since it is clearly less cumbersome to calculate v once and for all than to calculate $v_j(x)$ for every state you happen to pass through.

The "new" decision rule *(5a)* uncovers some amazing properties of the process. If $v > 0$, you should go on making observations until you get one, the value of which exceeds v, or until you are forced to stop, whichever occurs first. You should never bother about the number of possible remaining observations but just go ahead and behave as if nothing could possibly make you stop but the observation of a sufficiently large value, at least v. However, this event may fail to occur before you are actually forced to stop; you should then continue for as many periods (make as many observations) as you can and then quit the game, collecting the most valuable one of the prizes for the tickets you have bought (the largest observation you have made). Thus, you should exhaust your "budgeted resources" (buy all the tickets that you can buy) before stopping, unless you get a prize the value of which exceeds (or is at least equal to) what you would expect to get if you might continue buying tickets for ever. You should actually behave as if your optimal level of aspiration were equal to v, a constant, independent of <u>both</u> x and j. This will always lead to the same decisions as if you had used $v_j(x)$ for level of aspiration when in (j,x). Furthermore, since you might as well behave as if your level of aspiration were independent of j, you will reach the very same decisions even if, when you are in (j,x) for any $j \geqq 1$, you had used $v_k(x)$ for <u>any</u> $k \geqq 1$, $k \neq j$. This may also be seen directly from *(5)* since the equivalence holds for any $j \geqq 1$.

3.5.4 <u>Two questions</u>. Now at least two questions arise . First, will you ever need to calculate $v_j(x)$? To choose between continuing and stopping it is clearly sufficient to calculate v which is generally a much simpler task. Are there any situations where this is insufficient? Second, the above conclusions certainly indicate the existence of some fundamental difference between a process <u>with</u> recall and the corresponding one without. Could the same conclusions have been reached by some argument that is not based on having access to the explicit expression for $v_j(x)$?

The first question is the easier to answer and the answer will be in the affirmative. The two following examples indicate the kind of situation in which you will be helped by knowing the value of $v_j(x)$. In order to avoid some trivial cases, we assume that $v > 0$ and that $F(v-) \neq 0$. Hence, the process is a favourable one (see 2.4) and there is a positive probability that you will make an observation the value of which falls short of v in any single period. Note that $v_j(x)$ represents your expected net gain from not stopping when you are in (j,x).

Example 1. Suppose you are in (j,x), $j \geqq 1$, $x^+ < v$, and someone offers to buy you out of the process. What is the value of the smallest offer that you should accept? (Cf sale of patent rights etc) The answer is $v_j(x)$, since by selling your "rights to the process" you forego the possibility of continuing which is what you would have done otherwise. For the same reason, a buyer who evaluates the process in the same way as you do, will be quite prepared to offer you more than $v_j(x)$ if he is able to continue for longer than you (by (3)) but no more than $v_k(x)$, if k is the number of periods for which he can continue. However, even if he accepts and understands the "rules of the process", he may have another idea of the distribution function and of the values of the prizes. Then you are not going to be offered more than "$v_k(y)$" if he considers himself to be in state (k,y) after having bought you out, possibly calculated from some other distribution function than F.

Example 2. Suppose you are in (j,x), $j \geqq 0$, $x^+ < v$. What would it be worth to you to have k more periods at your disposal before being forced to stop? The answer is $v_{j+k}(x) - v_j(x)$, a quantity which by (3) is positive for every $k \geqq 1$. Note that unless $j = 0$, the extra periods may quite possibly never be used; the probability that you will make an observation the value of which exceeds v and hence stop after no more than j periods is $1 - F^j(v)$ (at least) which is positive (by A1P4 and A2P1). Nevertheless you should attach a positive value to obtaining the possibility of using one or several of them. After all, the probability that you will make use of the possibility is positive (since $F(v-) \neq 0$). The answer has some more properties that seem reasonable from an economic point of view: The more extra periods you can have, the more is it worth to you to have them. However, there is a definite least upper bound to this, namely $v - v_j(x)$. Also, the nearer you are to the point of forced stopping, the more is it worth to you to have access to a given number of extra periods. These properties are easily derived from *(3.4.23)* and *(3.4.24)*.

Thus the second question is settled. It is easy to imagine other situations in which you will be helped by knowing the value of $v_j(x)$; for example, you may also wish to know how sensitive the value of $v_j(x)$ is to changes in c, F or x. Thus, even if the second question must be ansered in the affirmative, it will sometimes be useful to know the explicit expression for $v_j(x)$.

As to the second question it will also have to be answered in the affirmative. In the next section it will be shown that the same conclusions can be reached by an argument which does not make use of the mathematical results derived in 3.4. In particular the argument is not based on having access to the explicit expression for $v_j(x)$. Actually, both the conclusions and the explicit expression for $v_j(x)$ can be derived from a (seemingly) less formal starting point, merely by making use of an (the?) essential difference between a process with recall and the corresponding one without.

This will all be done in the next section. The same things will thus be said once more. However, the way of saying them will be different, for now intuition enters, supported by our knowing what the result will be.

3.6 A MORE CONVERSATIONAL TREATMENT

3.6.1 The characteristics of an optimal decision rule and a proof for its existence. What distinquishes a process with recall from one without is this: Since previous results will never be lost to you if you continue, the value of what you will collect upon stopping cannot decrease as you continue from one state to another. This may obviously occur in a process without recall; there you have only recall to zero, not to any prizes having a positive value. However, in both cases you should always continue if the expected improvement of what you may collect from buying just one ticket and then stopping exceeds the cost of the ticket. These are our starting points.

Suppose you are in (j,x), $j \geqq 1$, in a process with recall. The expected improvement of what you may collect from buying just one more ticket is then $E\{\max(Y - x^+, 0)\}$ which is clearly non-negative and independent of j as it ought to be. Moreover, it is equal to $T_F(x^+)$ by *A1P1*. The cost of the ticket is c and by *A1P4* and *A2P1*, the sign of $T_F(x^+) - c$ is always equal to that of $v - x^+$, where v is uniquely defined by $T_F(v) = c$. Thus, if you are in (j,x), $j \geqq 1$, you should continue if $x^+ < v$.

This argument may be rendered even more conversational, should the need ever arise, for example by starting from some of the properties that "the expected improvement of what you may collect from buying just one more ticket and then stopping if you are in (j,x)" should have from an economic point of view. Just which properties to choose and how to proceed are strongly suggested by the contents of the previous paragraph.

So far, only half a decision rule has been produced, namely a sufficient condition for continuing. How should you behave if x^+ is greater than v or, which is the same thing, if your expected improvement from buying the next ticket and then stopping does not warrant the cost of the ticket? Perhaps you should go on. In fact, nothing has been said that would lead to the exclusion of the possibility that it might be favourable for you to buy just <u>two</u> tickets (or any number between 2 and j) and then to stop, even if buying just <u>one</u> ticket and then stopping is an unfavourable course of action.

However, none of these "simple" courses of action make use of the advantage that the sequential nature of the process has to offer. They are extremely rigid: " buy k tickets, no more and no less, and then stop"; even if you win the top prize (provided that there is one) with the <u>first</u> one of these tickets, you go on, stubbornly, buying $k - 1$ more tickets before stopping. Clearly, you can do better than that (on the average) by letting your choice of course of action in each stage depend on the values of the prizes already observed.

Now, suppose "buying just one ticket and then stopping" seems an unfavourable course of action. How about buying <u>at the most</u> two more tickets before stopping? This will seem worthwhile only if the second ticket comes from another lottery, one which, at the least, is so much "better" than the present one as to offset the expected loss incurred by the first ticket. But in this process, the construction of the lottery and the cost of a ticket (F and c) are unchanged from period to period. Since F and c never change, the expected loss incurred by the first ticket can never be expected to be recovered, even if you may go on for ever. Thus, if "buying just one ticket and then stopping" seems unfavourable to you, then you should not continue, that is, you should stop.

The expected change in your net gain from buying just one ticket and then stopping has already been found to be equal to $T_F(x^+) - c$, the sign of which is always the same as that of $v - x^+$. Thus, in a process with recall (and unchanged F and c) you should follow the decision rule:

$$(1) \qquad \text{If you are in } (j,x),\ j \geqq 1, \text{ then } \begin{cases} \underline{\text{continue}} & \text{if } x^+ < v \\ \underline{\text{stop}} & \text{if } x^+ > v \end{cases}$$

or one that is equivalent to it, that is, one that always tells you to do the same thing as *(1)* would have done. If $x^+ = v$, you should be indifferent to continuing or stopping, since your expected net gain will be the same, whether you stop or continue. If *(1)* is to be made complete, it will thus have to be divided into two rules, one which tells you to continue if $x^+ = v$ and one which tells you to stop under the same condition. This will be subsumed in *(1)* as it is formulated above. It will be a matter of taste, and circumstances outside the model, which one of the two variants you choose to follow. Your expected net gain will be the same under both of them, but the expected number of periods before you stop will differ, if (and only if) there is a positive probability of you drawing a ticket which has a prize value of exactly v.

Now, *(1)* is the only complete decision rule that can be derived from our starting points above (rules that are equivalent are considered as being the same rule). You will not accept a rule that violates these starting points, since one that conforms to them will give you a greater expected improvement of your net gain. Thus, any optimal decision rule must be equivalent to *(1)*.

Note that this is not the same thing as saying that *(1)* is the only optimal decision rule. There may not even exist an optimal decision rule. However, if there exists one, then *(1)*, including all rules equivalent to *(1)*, is the only optimal decision rule. For any finite value of j there certainly exists an optimal decision rule. This may be shown as follows.

Clearly there exists an optimal rule for a one-stage process, that is, for $j = 1$. Suppose there exists one for a k-stage process. Let $v_k(t)$ denote your expected net gain from participating (buying at least one ticket) in a k-stage process, starting in state (k,t), if you follow an optimal decision rule. Then $v_k(t)$ is well-defined for any t and no other decision rule can give you a greater expected net gain from participating. Now, imagine yourself in the beginning of a $k+1$-stage process, in state $(k + 1, x)$ for some x. Then, if you stop, you get x^+. If you continue you pay c and arrive in state $(k, \max(Y,x^+))$, which is the beginning of a k-stage process. Thus, the most you can expect to get from participating in a $(k+1)$-stage process, starting in $(k + 1, x)$, is $E\{\max[\max(Y,x^+), v_k(\max(Y,x^+))]\} - c$, which is a well-defined function of x. Denote it (formally) by $v_{k+1}(x)$. Then there exists an optimal decision rule for a $(k+1)$- stage process, namely this one: When in $(k + 1, x)$, continue if $x^+ \leqq v_{k+1}(x)$ and stop otherwise; from then on use an optimal rule for a k-stage process. Thus, if there exists an optimal decision rule for a k-stage process, then there also exists one for a $(k+1)$-stage process $(k \geqq 1)$. Since the if-clause is true for $k = 1$, the proposition follows by mathematical induction. Note also that $v_k(x)$ is formally identical to its namesake in *(3.3.8)*.

Then *(1)* is an optimal decision rule for any (finite) $j \geqq 1$. Thus, your expected net gain from participating (buying at least one ticket) in a j-stage process is exactly $v_j(x)$ if you start in (j,x) and follow *(1)* from the next stage and onwards. Using this result, we shall now derive an explicit expression for $v_j(x)$.

3.6.2 A derivation of an explicit expression for $v_j(x)$. From the above argument that led to *(1)* it is clear that $v_1(x) - x^+ = T_F(x^+) - c$ for any x, that is,

$$(2) \qquad v_1(x) = x^+ + T_F(x^+) - c \qquad x \in R$$

where the right hand side is equal to $E\{\max(Y,x^+)\} - c$ (see also *(3.3.7)*).

The number v, occuring in *(1)*, is such that, if you are in (j,v), $j \geqq 1$, then the expected improvement of your gross result from buying just one more ticket and then stopping is exactly offset by the cost of the ticket, that is, $E\{\max(Y - v, 0)\} = c$. Thus, v is such that if the values of all the lottery prizes were to be reduced by v, then you would be indifferent to participating or staying out of the process (see Section 2.4). Depending on the merits of the lottery, on the balance between F and c, the value of v may be equal to any real number. However, for any F and c it is uniquely determined by the relation above.

Suppose you are in state (j,x), $j \geqq 1$, and decide from the next stage on to follow *(1)*. Then, if $x^+ > v$ and if you actually continue, rule *(1)* will immediately tell you to stop after you have bought the ticket, so you will in fact behave as if j were equal to 1. Hence,

$$(3) \qquad v_j(x) = v_1(x), \; x^+ > v, \; j \geqq 1$$

This includes the case when v is negative.

There remains to determine $v_j(x)$ for $x^+ \leqq v$ and $j > 1$. One way of doing this is by solving the difference equation *(3.3.8)*. This was done in Section 3.4. Another way is suggested by Example 2 of Section 3.5, making use of *(1)* and the economic interpretation of $v_{j+1}(x) - v_j(x)$. This way will pursued below. Still another method is suggested by *(1)* and the interpretation (definition) of $v_j(x)$ given above. That method will be pursued subsequently (in 3.6.3).

Suppose you are in (j,x), $j \geqq 1$ and $x^+ \leqq v$. Assume further that you follow that variant of rule *(1)* which tells you to continue if $x^+ \leqq v$ and to stop otherwise. You will then continue and your expected net gain from doing so is equal to $v_j(x)$. How much would it be worth to you to have one more period at your disposal before you are forced to stop? If you had, you would now be in state $(j + 1, x)$ instead of (j,x), but you would still continue. Thus, the expected value of having one more period at your disposal is equal to $v_{j+1}(x) - v_j(x)$.

The possibility of buying one more ticket will be clearly of no value to you unless you make use of it, and unless the extra ticket wins a prize, the value of which is greater than that of any ticket bought previously and also greater than x^+. You will buy the extra ticket only if rule *(1)* has not told you to stop before you can buy it, that is, only if none of the j tickets preceding it has won a prize valued in excess of v.

Let Z_k denote the value of the most valuable of the prizes for k tickets drawn independently of one another and with replacement from the lottery. Then $Z_k = \max(Y_1, Y_2, \ldots, Y_k)$ where the Y:s denote the values of the respective tickets, all of them being independent random variables having the same distribution function, F. Thus Z_k has the distribution function F^k, $k \geqq 1$ (see A1.3).

Let U denote the improvement of your (gross) gain, achievable by you having the possibility of buying an extra ticket at the end of a j-stage process. Let Y denote the prize value of the extra ticket. Then U will be zero, if <u>either</u> $x^+ > v$ (in which case you stop where you are) <u>or</u> $Z_j > v$ (in which case rule *(1)* will have stopped you before you have bought the extra ticket) <u>or</u> $Y \leqq \max(Z_j, x^+)$ (in which case the prize value of the extra ticket is no greater than that of one of those bought previously). In the opposite case, the improvement of your gross result will be $Y - \max(Z_j, x^+)$, which is clearly positive, as it ought to be; in a process with recall, your gain can never decrease. Thus,

$$(4) \qquad U = \begin{cases} 0 & \text{, if } x^+ > v \text{ or } Z_j > v \text{ or } Y \leqq \max(Z_j, x^+) \\ Y - \max(Z_j, x^+), & \text{if } x^+ \leqq v \text{ and } Z_j \leqq v \text{ and } Y > \max(Z_j, x^+) \end{cases}$$

Since Y and Z_j are independent random variables having known distribution functions F and F^j, respectively, the expected value of U can be written as

$$(5) \qquad E\{U\} = \int_D [y - \max(t, x^+)] dF(y) dF^j(t)$$

where $D = \{(y,t) \mid \max(t,x^+) \leqq v \wedge y > \max(t,x^+)\}$ so that *(5)* can be written as

$$\text{(6)}\qquad E\{U\} = \int_{-\infty}^{v}\left[\int_{\max(t,x^+)}^{\infty} [y - \max(t,x^+)]dF(y)\right]d[F^j(t)] =$$

$$= \int_{-\infty}^{v} T_F(\max(t,x^+))d[F^j(t)] =$$

$$= T_F(x^+)F^j(x^+) + \int_{x^+}^{v} T_F(t)d[F^j(t)]$$

The above second equality follows from noting that the inner integral in the expression preceding it, stands for $E\{\max[Y - \max(t,x^+), 0]\}$ which makes *A1P1(ii)* directly applicable. The last equality is obtained by splitting up the preceding integral into two, one with $(-\infty,x^+]$ as its domain of integration and the other with $(x^+,v]$, the latter of which remains to be developed.

This is done by straight-forward partial integration (Cf. *A1P11*). Let

$$u = T_F(t) \qquad\qquad v = F^j(t)$$

$$du = (F(t) - 1)dt \qquad\qquad dv = dF^j(t)$$

Then the integral becomes

$$T_F(v)F^j(v) - T_F(x^+)F^j(x^+) + \int_{x^+}^{v} F^j(t)(1 - F(t))dt$$

so that, finally, $E\{U\}$ can be rewritten as

$$\text{(7)}\qquad E\{U\} = \int_{x^+}^{v} F^j(t)(1 - F(t))dt + T_F(v)F^j(v)$$

Now, the cost for achieving this expected improvement of your gross result will clearly be zerc if the extra observation is never used and otherwise c, that is, with probability $P\{Z_j \leqq v\}$. Thus, the expected cost is $cP\{Z_j \leqq v\} = T_F(v)F^j(v)$, the last term in *(7)*!

Hence, if you are in (j,x), $j \geqq 1$ and $x^+ \leqq v$, your expected net gain from having one more period at your disposal before you are forced to stop is equal to the integral in *(7)*, that is,

$$(8) \qquad v_{j+1}(x) - v_j(x) = \int_{x^+}^{v} F^j(t)(1 - F(t))dt \qquad x^+ \leqq v,\ j \geqq 1$$

By *(2)*, $v_1(x)$ has already been determined, so $v_j(x)$ can be arrived at by use of *(8)* and noting that $v_j(x) = v_1(x) + \sum_{k=1}^{j-1} [v_{k+1}(x) - v_k(x)]$. Then

$$(9) \qquad v_j(x) - v_1(x) = \sum_{k=1}^{j-1} \int_{x^+}^{v} F^k(t)(1 - F(t))dt =$$

$$= \int_{x^+}^{v} (1 - F(t)) \sum_{k=1}^{j-1} F^k(t)dt =$$

$$= \int_{x^+}^{v} F(t)(1 - F^{j-1}(t))dt =$$

$$= \int_{x^+}^{v} (1 - F^j(t))dt - \int_{x^+}^{v} (1 - F(t))dt =$$

$$= T_{F^j}(x^+) - T_{F^j}(v) - (T_F(x^+) - c)$$

the last term (within parantheses) of which is equal to $v_1(x) - x^+$ by *(2)*. Thus

$$(10) \qquad v_j(x) = x^+ + T_{F^j}(x^+) - T_{F^j}(v) \qquad x^+ \leqq v,\ j \geqq 1$$

which together with *(2)* and *(3)* once again yields the expression *(3.5.2)*, derived by other means in Section 3.4.

3.6.3 <u>An alternative derivation</u>. As we said before, still another method of deriving an expression for $v_j(x)$ is suggested by *(1)* and the interpretation (definition) of $v_j(x)$ given earlier. Thus, *(1)* is known to be an optimal decision rule, and your expected net gain from participating in a j-stage process is exactly $v_j(x)$ if you start in (j,x) and follow an optimal decision rule (such as *(1)* or any rule equivalent to *(1)*) from the next stage and onwards. This method will now be pursued.

The case $x^+ > v$ is covered by *(2)* and *(3)*, so only the case $x^+ \leqq v$ need be considered. There is then an optimal decision rule that will actually tell you to continue when you are in (j,x), $j \geqq 1$, so $v_j(x)$ denotes your expected net result from participating in the process, if you follow *(1)* all the time.

Thus, suppose $x^+ \leqq v$ and that you follow that variant of *(1)* which tells you to continue if $x^+ = v$. You will eventually stop, however, either after having made an observation, the value of which is greater than v, or after having made all j observations at your disposal, whichever event occurs first. Let N denote the number of periods for which you continue if you follow the above rule and if you stop after j periods, unless the rule has previously told you to stop. Then N is a random variable the value of which will be an integer between 1 and j.

Consider the event $\{N = n\}$ for some integer n such that $2 \leqq n \leqq j-1$. This event occurs if and only if rule *(1)* tells you to stop after exactly n periods, which will occur if and only if the value of the n:th observation turns out to be greater than v while those of the $n - 1$ preceding observations are at most equal to v. Thus, $\{N = n\} = \{Y_n > v$ and $Z_{n-1} \leqq v\}$ in the notation introduced above (see 3.6.2), for $2 \leqq n \leqq j-1$. For $n = 1$ the event is equal to $\{Y_1 > v\}$.

Clearly the event $\{N > j-1\}$ is equal to $\{N = j\}$, since you will always stop after j observations unless you have stopped **previous**ly Also, for $1 \leqq n \leqq j-1$, the event $\{N > n\}$ occurs if and only if the values of the n first observations are at most equal to v. Thus $\{N > n\} = \{Z_n \leqq v\}$, $1 \leqq n \leqq j-1$. Since you will always make at least one observation, the event $\{N > 0\}$ is certain to occur. On the other hand, since you will never make more than j observations, the event $\{N > j\}$ will never occur.

It was shown earlier than Z_n has the distribution function F^n, $n \geqq 1$. It then follows from the above that

$$(11) \qquad P\{N > n\} = \begin{cases} 1 & n < 1 \\ F^n(v) & 1 \leqq n < j \\ 0 & j \leqq n \end{cases}$$

Note that $P\{N = n\} = P\{N > n-1\} - P\{N > n\}$, so that *(11)* also yields the probability function for N. The expression for $P\{N = n\}$ obtained in this way agrees with that obtained by making use of the above discussion of the events $\{N = n\}$, and the fact that Y_n and Z_{n-1} are independent random variables.

Then $E\{N\}$ can be determined, noting that N is a non-negative integer-valued random variable (see *(A1.1.2)* and *(A1.1.7)*), and we get

$$(12) \qquad E\{N\} = \sum_{n=0}^{\infty} P\{N > n\} = \sum_{n=0}^{j-1} F^n(v) = \frac{1 - F^j(v)}{1 - F(v)} \qquad j \geqq 1$$

where v is a well-defined number (*A2P1*) and $F(v)$ is less than 1 (*A1P4*) Hence, $E\{N\}$ is well-defined for any positive j, and even for j infinite, since the sum involved converges. For the moment it is rather $E\{cN\}$ that is of interest, the expected cost of the observations that you will make before stopping, if you follow rule *(1)* in a j-stage process. Since $E\{cN\} = cE\{N\}$, its value is easily determined by use of *(12)*.

Let R_N denote the value of what you collect upon stopping, if you stop after exactly N observations. Since you will always collect at least x^+ which is non-negative, R_N is a non-negative random variable and its expected value may be determined in a similar way as that used above for N. However, R_N is actually a whole set of random variables, one for each value of N, so the determination of its expected value will have to proceed in two steps. First, let the value of N be given, say $N = n$, and determine the conditional expectation of R_N, given that $N = n$. This may be accomplished by use of *(13)*:

$$(13) \qquad E\{R_N | N = n\} = \int_0^\infty P\{R_N > t | N = n\} dt \qquad 1 \leq n \leq j$$

Then, since $P\{N = n\}$ is known, $E\{R_N\}$ is determined by *(14)*:

$$(14) \qquad E\{R_N\} = \sum_{n=1}^{j} E\{R_N | N = n\} P\{N = n\}$$

From the context of the problem it is clear that R_n (the value of what you collect upon stopping if you stop after n periods) is equal to Y_n, if $1 \leq n \leq j-1$, and to $\max(Z_j, x^+)$ otherwise, that is, if $n = j$. Then, for $2 \leq n \leq j-1$, $P\{R_N > t | N = n\} = P\{Y_n > t | Y_n > v \text{ and } Z_{n-1} \leq v\} =$
$= [P\{Y_n > t \text{ and } Y_n > v \text{ and } Z_{n-1} \leq v\} / P\{Y_n > t \text{ and } Z_{n-1} \leq v\}] =$
$= P\{Y_n > \max(t,v)\} / P\{Y_n > t\}$, since Y_n and Z_{n-1} are independent. The last expression is true for $n = 1$ as well. Thus, for $1 \leq n \leq j-1$, we have

$$(15) \qquad P\{R_N > t | N = n\} = \begin{cases} 1 & t < v \\ \dfrac{1 - F(t)}{1 - F(v)} & t \geq v \end{cases}$$

For $n = j$, $P\{R_N \leq t | N = n\} = P\{\max(Z_j, x^+) \leq t | Z_{j-1} \leq v\} =$
$= P\{Y_j \leq t \text{ and } Z_{j-1} \leq t \text{ and } x^+ \leq t | Z_{j-1} \leq v\} =$

$$= \frac{P\{Y_j \leq t \text{ and } Z_{j-1} \leq \min(t,v) \text{ and } x^+ \leq t\}}{P\{Z_{j-1} \leq v\}} = \begin{cases} 0 & t < x^+ \\ \dfrac{F(t) F^{j-1}(\min(t,v))}{F^{j-1}(v)}, & t \geq x^+ \end{cases}$$

which yields

$$(16) \qquad P\{R_N > t | N = j\} = \begin{cases} 1 & t < x^+ \\ 1 - \dfrac{F^j(t)}{F^{j-1}(v)} & x^+ \leq t < v \\ 1 - F(t) & v \leq t \end{cases}$$

Then, by *(13)* and *(15)*, it is seen that

$$(17) \qquad E\{R_N | N = n\} = v + \frac{T_F(v)}{1 - F(v)} \qquad 1 \leq n \leq j-1$$

and similarly, by *(13)* and *(16)*,

$$(18) \qquad E\{R_N | N = j\} = x^+ + \int_{x^+}^{v} (1 - \frac{F^j(t)}{F^{j-1}(v)})dt + T_F(v) =$$

$$= v - [F(v)]^{-(j-1)} \int_{x^+}^{v} F^j(t)dt + T_F(v)$$

Note that by *(17)* the expected value of what you collect upon stopping, provided that you will not be forced to stop, is independent of the number of periods for which you continue. This will be utilized in the next section for proving the existence of an optimal decision rule for an infinite process of this kind. Clearly an infinite process has the characteristic that you will never be forced to stop, so the expected value of what you collect upon stopping if you participate in such a process and follow rule *(1)*, is equal to the right hand side of *(17)*(see also *(14)*).

For a j-stage process, given *(17)*, *(18)*, and *(14)*, $E\{R_N\}$ is simply the sum of $E\{R_N | 1 \leq N \leq j-1\}P\{N \leq j-1\}$ and $E\{R_N | N = j\}P\{N = j\}$. Thus, by *(11)*,

$$(19) \qquad E\{R_N\} = (v + \frac{T_F(v)}{1 - F(v)})(1 - F^{j-1}(v)) + E\{R_N | N = j\}F^{j-1}(v) =$$

$$= v - \int_{x^+}^{v} F^j(t)dt + T_F(v)\left[\frac{1 - F^{j-1}(v)}{1 - F(v)} + F^{j-1}(v)\right]$$

After reduction, the last expression within square brackets in *(19)* is seen to be equal to $E\{N\}$ by *(12)*. Furthermore, $T_F(v) = c$ by definition (*A2D1*), so the last term in *(19)* is equal to $E\{cN\}$, the expected cost of the tickets you buy before stopping. By adding and subtracting x^+ to the remainder of the last expression in *(19)*, it can be rewritten as $x^+ + \int_{x^+}^{v} (1 - F^j(t))dt$, which gives it a more familiar look. Thus,

$$(20) \qquad E\{R_N\} = x^+ + T_{F^j}(x^+) - T_{F^j}(v) + E\{cN\}$$

Now, $E\{R_N - cN\}$, that is, $E\{R_N\} - E\{cN\}$, represents your expected net gain from participating in a j-stage process, starting in (j,x), $j \geqq 1$ and $x^+ \leqq v$, if you follow rule *(1)*. On the other hand, the very same expected value was previously defined as $v_j(x)$. Thus, by *(20)*,

$$(21) \qquad v_j(x) = x^+ + T_{F^j}(x^+) - T_{F^j}(v) \qquad x^+ \leqq v,\ j \geqq 1$$

which is *(10)* once again.

The promise made at the end of Section 3.5 has now been kept. One more question remains to be settled, however: Does there exist an optimal decision rule for an infinite process of this kind? If it does, then it is rule *(1)*, that much is known. But it is one thing to describe a unicorn and quite another matter to show that one exists. In the next section we shall prove the existence, not of a unicorn but of an optimal decision rule for a process in which you will never be forced to stop.

3.7 THE EXISTENCE OF AN OPTIMAL DECISION RULE FOR AN INFINITE PROCESS

In the preceding section it was found that the decision rule

$$(1) \qquad \text{If you are in } (j,x),\ j \geqq 1, \quad \begin{cases} \underline{\text{stop}}, & \text{if } x^+ > v \\ \underline{\text{continue}}, & \text{if } x^+ \leqq v \end{cases}$$

is an optimal decision rule for any finite process, that is, one in which you will be forced to stop after a finite number of periods unless you have not stopped earlier. Moreover, from the argument of **3.6.1**, we may conclude that *(1)* is an optimal decision rule even for an infinite process, provided that one exists for such a process. The purport of the following argument is to show that this is indeed the case.

An infinite process is one in which you will never be forced to stop. No matter how many observations you have made, the "number" of observations remaining before you are forced to stop will then always be the same. As on the high seas, you are always at the same distance from the horizon. Thus, the state of the process is always exhaustively characterized by the value of the largest observation you have so far made, that is, by x; j need never inter into the state description.

A decision rule is a rule which tells you what to do under all conceivable circumstances. More formally, it is a function which maps each circumstance on an action. Here, the set of actions, "what to do", has exactly two elements: stop and continue. The set of circumstances is the set of states of the process which may be taken to be equivalent to the set of real numbers, R. Then any decision rule for this process will be of the form:

$$\text{(2)} \qquad \text{If you are in state } x\text{, then} \quad \begin{matrix} \underline{\text{stop}}, & \text{if } x^+ \in S \\ \underline{\text{continue}}, & \text{if } x^+ \notin S \end{matrix}$$

where x is a real number and S is some subset of R.(The sign $\notin$ means "does not belong to".) For example, rule *(1)* may be written on this form by letting S be the set $\{t | t^+ > v\}$. Since the set of actions has only two elements, *(2)* may be condensed into

$$\text{(3)} \qquad \underline{\text{stop}}, \text{ iff } x^+ \in S$$

("iff" stands for "if and only if") where it is understood that the rule tells you to go on if x^+ does not belong to S.

An optimal decision rule is one which, if you follow it, will give you an expected net gain from the process, the value of which cannot be improved upon by any other decision rule. Rule *(1)* is an obvious candidate for the title. By *(3.6.17)* and *(3.6.12)*, if $v \geqq 0$, your expected net result from participating in the process if you follow *(1)* is v, which is a well-defined number. If there is a better rule (in the above sense), then it is to be found among the rules *(3)* for some shrewd choice of S. There are simply no other rules to choose from, so if none of those is better, then rule *(1)* is in fact an optimal decision rule.

To put it mildly there is quite a number of ways of choosing S. However, some ways are obviously bad. By recognizing these and excluding them from further discussion, there is some hope of arriving at a more manageable set of rules, the set of possible candidates.

Some obviously bad rules are those which never tell you to stop. If you follow one of those, you will go on for ever, paying c for each period that you go on but never collecting a thing. Thus, S should be such that the set $\{x|x^+ \in S\}$ contains at least one element, that is, S must have at least one non-negative element. Moreover, since x^+ is always non-negative, there is no loss in generality in restrictning S to be a subset of the set of non-negative real numbers, R^+. Thus, S is bounded from below. Now the set of candidates has been reduced to rules of the form

(4) <u>stop</u>, iff $x^+ \in S \qquad S \subset R^+,\ S \neq \emptyset$

where $\emptyset$ denotes the empty set.

Suppose $y \in S$, $y \geqq 0$. Such a number certainly exists, since S has at least one non-negative element. However, for all we know, y is the only element of S, and this seems to yield a rather strange decision rule considering the nature of the problem. Surely, if you are content with collecting y upon stopping, then you should be quite as content (if not more) with collecting z, if z is greater than y. After all, if it is only y that you want, you could always throw away the difference after having collected z. So, a rule which tells you to stop when you are in state y but to continue when you are in state z, where z is some number greater than y, is also an obviously bad rule. Furthermore, since S is bounded from below, it has a greatest lower bound, inf S. Let inf$S$ be denoted by t. Then S must be of the form $\{y|y > t\}$ or $\{y|y \geqq t\}$ where t is some non-negative real number.

Now the set of candidates has been reduced to rules of the form

$$(5) \qquad \underline{\text{stop}}, \text{ iff } x^+ > t \qquad t \geqq 0$$

or

$$(5') \qquad \underline{\text{stop}}, \text{ iff } x^+ \geqq t \qquad t \geqq 0$$

If your expected net gain from following a particular one of these rules (for some particular value of t, say t_0) cannot be improved upon by following one of the other rules of this type (for some value of t different from t_0), then there exists an optimal decision rule for the process (namely the one for which $t = t_0$). The set of rules defined by *(5)* will be examined first.

Let t be such that $F(t) = 1$. With probability one you will then continue for ever, so those rules are no good. Let t be such that $F(t) < 1$. Then the arguments of the preceding section apply again (see 3.6.3). Thus, by substituting t for v in *(3.6.17)*, we find that the expected value of what you collect upong stopping is

$$(6) \qquad E\{R_N\} = t + \frac{T_F(t)}{1 - F(t)}$$

Similarly, by *(3.6.12)* the expected cost of the observations you make before stopping is found to be

$$(7) \qquad cE\{N\} = \frac{c}{1 - F(t)}$$

For each value of $t \geqq 0$, let $W(t)$ denote your expected net gain from following rule *(5)*. Then $W(t) = E\{R_N\} - cE\{N\}$ and by *(6)* and *(7)*,

$$(8) \qquad W(t) = t + \frac{T_F(t) - c}{1 - F(t)} \qquad t \geqq 0, \; F(t) < 1$$

Since $c = T_F(v)$, (8) can be rewritten as

$$(9) \qquad W(t) = t + \int_t^v (1 - F(s))ds/(1 - F(t)) \qquad t \geqq 0,\ F(t) < 1$$

Suppose $v \geqq 0$. Then $W(v) = v$ and for $t \neq v$

$$(10) \qquad W(t) \leqq t + (v - t)(1 - F(t))/(1 - F(t)) = v$$

which implies

$$(11) \qquad W(t) \leqq W(v) \qquad t \geqq 0,\ v \geqq 0$$

If v is negative, (10) still holds, which means that $W(t) \leqq v < 0$ for all $t \geqq 0$ so you should stop, whatever state you happen to be in. This is precisely what rule (1) would have told you to do, so no rule is better than (1) if $v < 0$. Then, by (11), we find that there exists an optimal decision rule for an infinite process, namely,

(12) <u>stop</u> iff $x^+ > v$

The same argument (with the obvious modifications) goes through for rules of type (5'). Thus,

(12') <u>stop</u> iff $x^+ \geqq v$

is also an optimal decision rule.

3.8 MYOPIC DECISION RULES

If you follow an optimal decision rule in a process of this kind (whether with or without recall) you are taking the <u>whole</u> future into account. One such decision rule for a process with recall is, by definition,

(1) If you are in (j,x), $j \geqq 1$, then $\begin{array}{ll} \underline{\text{stop}} & \text{if } x^+ > v_j(x) \\ \underline{\text{continue}} & \text{if } x^+ \leqq v_j(x) \end{array}$

since $v_j(x)$ is your greatest possible net gain from continuing when you are in (j,x), whatever decision rule you choose to follow. However, we have also found that the sign of $v_j(x) - x^+$ is always the same as that of $v - x^+$, whatever be x or j (see 3.5.3), so the decision rule

(2) If you are in (j,x), $j \geqq 1$, then $\begin{array}{ll} \underline{\text{stop}} & \text{if } x^+ > v \\ \underline{\text{continue}} & \text{if } x^+ \leqq v \end{array}$

will always tell you to choose the same action as (1) would have done. Moreover, (1) and (2) are both of them equivalent to

(3) If you are in (j,x), $j \geqq 1$, then $\begin{array}{ll} \underline{\text{stop}} & \text{if } x^+ > v_k(x) \\ \underline{\text{continue}} & \text{if } x^+ \leqq v_k(x) \end{array}$

for <u>any</u> $k \geqq 1$. As we found before, it looks as if you need not bother about the number of remaining observations when you choose your level of aspiration. In economic terms this means that what is good in the short run is also good in the long run (and *vice versa*). It certainly seems worthwhile to investigate the conditions under which this is true.

In particular, if you use $v_1(x)$ for your level of aspiration when in (j,x), $j \geqq 1$, you act as if the next observation were to be the last. You are taking only the <u>immediate</u> future into account, disregarding the consequences of continuing beyond the next observation. Such behaviour is called <u>myopic</u> and the corresponding decision rule is called a <u>myopic decision rule</u>. Thus, (3) is a myopic decision rule for $k=1$. Moreover, since (3) is equivalent to (1) and (2), a myopic decision rule is in fact optimal for a process with recall, whether forced stopping will eventually occur or not.

Let us see if some similar result can be shown to hold for a process <u>without</u> recall. Your optimal level of aspiration is then v_j when you are in (j,x), $j \geqq 1$ (determined by (2.3.5)) and the myopic level is

v_1. As in 2.5 we disregard such processes in which you should make at the most one observation; then myopic behaviour is optimal by definition. For all other processes we have found that $v_j > v_1 > 0$, $j \geqq 1$ and $\lim_{j\to\infty} v_j = v$ (see Table 1 of 2.4) where v is the same as in *(2)*. Thus, if you are in (j,x), $j > 1$ and $v_1 < x^+ < v_j$ a myopic decision rule will tell you to stop whereas the "best" thing to do is to continue.

However, it may be impossible (probability zero) to reach such a state. Then $F(v_j-) - F(v_1) = 0$ for each relevant value of j. We conclude: If $F(v_j-) \neq F(v_1)$ for some value of j, then a myopic decision rule will not be optimal for a process without recall.

Thus, a myopic decision rule is optimal for a process <u>with</u> recall whereas in general this is not the case for one <u>without</u>.

3.9 CONCLUSION

We have now studied the consequences of changing the assumptions of the basic model in such a way that what you collect upon stopping is <u>any one</u> of the prizes for your previous tickets; you have <u>recall</u> to any previous observation. An optimal decision rule is then

(1) If you are in (j,x), $j \geqq 1$, then <u>stop</u> if $x^+ > v_j(x)$, <u>continue</u> if $x^+ \leqq v_j(x)$

where $v_j(x)$ can be calculated for any (j,x) by use of *(3.5.2)* given only F and c. For any fixed x, the properties of monotonicity and convergence of $v_j(x)$ are the same as those of v_j. Moreover, $\lim_{j\to\infty} v_j(x) = \lim v_j = v$, so the interpretations given to v_j and v in Chapter 2 could be transferred to $v_j(x)$ and v of the present case.

In order to justify the interpretation of v as your optimal level of aspiration in a favourable infinite process ($v > 0$), it was proved in 3.7 that there exists an optimal decision rule for such a process.

Your expected net gain from following such a rule is v, and the rule is good for a process without recall as well.[1]

Some important differences between the models have been discovered. We found in 3.5.3 that the decision rule *(1)* is equivalent to the one obtained by substituting v (or $v_k(x)$ for any $k \geqq 1$) for $v_j(x)$. Thus a myopic decision rule (see 3.8) is always optimal for a process with recall whereas in general this is not the case for one without. Moreover, since v may now safely be interpreted as your expected net gain from participating in a favourable infinite process, the following was found to be an optimal way of behaving in a favourable process with recall: Continue until you are forced to stop or until you have made an observation the value of which exceeds what you would expect to get from an infinite process, whichever event occurs first.

Let us return to the two features of a process <u>without</u> recall which made us modify the basic model on this point. One of them is this (see 2.5):

- At each decision point the expected value of continuing is independent of the value of stopping.

This is <u>not</u> true for a process <u>with</u> recall; $v_j(x)$ depends on x as well as on j. (This must not be confused with the fact that you may as well use v, which is independent of both j and x, for your level of aspiration; $v_j(x)$ remains your expected net gain from continuing if you follow an optimal decision rule, whatever be the shape of this rule.) In this respect the modification was successful.

The other one is this:

- You should participate (buy at least one ticket) in a lottery of this kind if and <u>only if</u> it is favourable to participate on a one-period basis, i.e. on the condition that you may only buy <u>one</u> ticket.

This is true for a process <u>with</u> recall as well. It seems to be due to the fact that F and c never change as you continue: The prospects of

---

[1] The proof is inspired by Radner(1964, pp 212-215).

the immediate future are good if and only if those of the whole future are.

So, further modifications are called for. In Chapter 5 we shall examine the consequences of letting c, the cost of an observation, vary as you continue. However, before leaving the basic models we shall study their properties under the further assumption that you want to maximize the expected present value of your net gain, using a positive rate of return for discounting future costs and rewards. This will be done in the next chapter, the results of which will then be applied to the more general models of Chapter 5.

4 The Basic Models with Discounting

4.1 INTRODUCTION

So far the value of an observation has been considered the same no matter when the observation is made. On the other hand, due to the positive cost of each observation, your actual net gain from participating is less the more observations that have to be made before a "good one" materializes (as compared to observing the same value in some earlier period). However, this is a rather crude way of incorporating time-preference, since it fails to discriminate between high and low values of the observations, the cost of delay being independent of the value observed; it certainly violates the assumptions of time-preference inherent in most methods of evaluating investments.

An easy remedy for this is to apply the idea of using a constant positive rate of return per value unit and time period for evaluating the benefits foregone by the value appearing later rather than sooner (and the benefits obtained by the cost of each future observation except the next one being payed for then rather than now). This can also conveniently be fitted into the models of the two preceding chapters and the consequences of doing so will now be examined. The standard for comparing decision rules will thus be the expected present value of your net gain from participating in the process, and we get the "old" models as special cases by using a zero rate of return. The treatment will be less detailed than that of the preceding chapters, the methods and results of which are assumed to be known.

4.2 ASSUMPTIONS AND NOTATION

For detailed statements of the assumptions, see the corresponding sections of the preceding chapters. As for notation, the state of the process is still characterized by the ordered pair (j,x), where j stands for the number of periods remaining before you will be forced to stop and x stands for the value of the observation that you would collect upon stopping unless you prefer to collect nothing.

If you continue, you first pay c and then you make the next observation, the value of which will be known to you one time period later. Its nominal value is a random variable, Y, having the distribution function F. Its present value will be qY, where $q = 1/(1 + r)$ is the discount factor corresponding to a rate of return of $100r$ % per value unit and time period. The rate of return is assumed to be non-negative so q is a real number between zero and one, that is, $r \geqq 0$ and $0 < q \leqq 1$.

You want to behave so as to maximize the expected present value of your net gain from participating in the process. The problem is to find a decision rule by which this can be achieved (and we know that one exists).

Let $U(j,x)$ denote the value to you of being in state (j,x) if you follow an optimal decision rule. Then

$$(1) \qquad U(j,x) = \max\begin{Bmatrix}\text{Value of stopping} \\ \text{Expected net present value of continuing}\end{Bmatrix}$$

which is the analogue of $V(j,x)$ of (2.2.1) and (3.3.2). And now to the point.

4.3 THE BASIC MODEL

4.3.1 Basic results. In a process without recall, the situation can be described as in Figure 1.

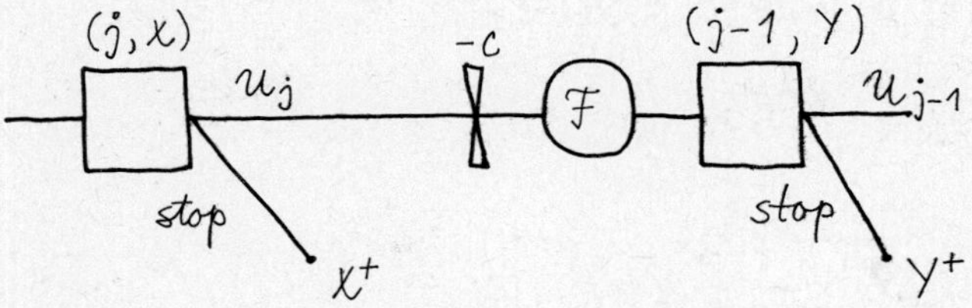

Figure 1 *A decision tree for a process without recall*

From left to right: When you are in (j,x), $j \geq 1$, you have the choice of either stopping, which gives x^+, or continuing, the expected net present value of which is denoted by u_j (the analogue of v_j of Chapter 2). Then (see *(4.2.1)* and *(2.2.5)*).

$$(2) \qquad U(j,x) = \max(x^+, u_j)$$

If you choose to continue, you have to pay c at once. Then chance takes over (distribution function F) and sends you to state $(j - 1, Y)$ where you arrive one period later. Then your expected net present value of continuing from (j,x) becomes (see *(2.2.4)*)

$$(3) \qquad u_j = - c + qE\{U(j - 1, Y)\}$$

which by *(2)* may be rewritten as (see *(2.2.6)*)

$$(4) \qquad u_j = - c + qE\{\max(Y^+, u_{j-1})\}$$

This can also be "read off" Figure 1 above, noting that u_{j-1} is itself a net present value but discounted to "time-point" $j-1$, whereas c refers to time-point j. Also, at each decision point, of the two courses of action that are open to you, you choose the more favourable. In the end you are forced to stop, however, a case that is incorporated in *(4)* by <u>defining</u> u_0 to be equal to zero. As before, this is just a formal definition; u_0 is not to be given an interpretation such as that of u_j for $j \geqq 1$.

So, given c and F, the distribution function of Y, the sequence of numbers u_j, $j \geqq 0$, is uniquely determined by the recursive relation

$$(5)\quad \begin{cases} u_j = qE\{\max(Y^+, u_{j-1})\} - c & j \geqq 1 \\ u_0 = 0 \end{cases}$$

which reduces to *(2.2.8)* for $q = 1$ as it ought to do.

By the same argument that led to *(2.3.5)* it is seen that *(5)* can be rewritten as

$$(6)\quad u_j = \begin{cases} qT_F(0) - c & u_{j-1} \leqq 0 \\ q[u_{j-1} + T_F(u_{j-1})] - c & u_{j-1} > 0 \end{cases} \qquad j \geqq 1$$

keeping in mind that u_0 is equal to zero. For $q = 1$, *(6)* is equivalent to *(2.3.5)*. Thus, $u_j \equiv v_j$ for $q = 1$, as is to be required.

The properties of monotonicity and convergence are summarized by the counterparts of the equivalences *(2.3.16)* and *(2.3.17)*.(for a proof, see *A3P8*):

$$(7)\qquad u > \max(0,u_1) \iff (u > u_{j+1} > u_j\ ,\ j \geqq 1) \wedge \lim_{j\to\infty} u_j = u$$

$$(8)\qquad u \leqq \max(0,u_1) \iff u_j = u_1 \qquad j \geqq 1$$

where u is uniquely defined by the equation (see *(6)*, *A2D2*, and *A2P3*):

$$(9)\qquad u = q(u + T_F(u)) - c$$

which reduces to *A2D1* for $q = 1$ as it ought to do.

Most of what was said about v_j in 2.3 is then seen to hold true for u_j as well (with some obvious changes in notation). Thus, all properties of monotonicity and convergence are immediately carried over (for proofs, see A2 and A3). However, the numerical values of u_j and v_j and those of their limits will differ, depending on the value of q.

4.3.2 <u>Interpretations and comparisons.</u> Suppose you use a positive rate of discount, that is, $r > 0$ and $q < 1$. How will u_j differ from v_j? It follows from *(6)* that $v_1 \leqq 0$ implies $u_1 < 0$, and hence $u_j = u_1 < 0$, $j \geqq 1$ (*A3P1*). Thus, using the terminology of Section 2.4, a process that does not look favourable without discounting is definitely unfair if discounting is introduced. In all other cases it is true that $u_j < v_j$, $j \geqq 1$ (*A3P9*). Thus, a process that looks favourable without discounting will look less favourable if discounting is introduced. It will even seem unfavourable for sufficiently large rates of return. In these cases then $(v_1 > 0)$, you should have a <u>lower</u> level of aspiration at <u>each</u> decision point as compared to the situation without descounting.

Suppose still that you use a positive rate of discount. Then for the case where $\lim_{j\to\infty} u_j = u$, *(7)*, we have $0 < u < v$ by *A3P2* and *A2P5*. Moreover, u is a strictly decreasing function of r (*A2P7*). Thus, the expected value of continuing <u>without</u> a resource limit (no forced stopping) is less with discounting than without it; the larger the discount rate, the smaller is the value.

As for interpretations most of what was said about v_j in Section 2.4 holds true for u_j as well since it is based on properties of monotonicity and convergence. Some modifications of the arguments must be made, however, due to the explicit consideration that must now be given to the time of occurence of various consequences. These modifications will now be made.

The number v has been given two interpretations, one of which does not immediately carry over to u: If v_1 is positive, v is the amount by which the value of each prize of the lottery must be reduced for you to be indifferent to participating or not participating. Thus, $E\{(Y - v)^+\} = c$. However, the corresponding number in the case with discounting is not equal to u (but in one case, u is the present value of the corresponding number; see below).

Suppose u_1 is positive, that is, $qE\{Y^+\} > c$. Let p denote a number that can be given the same interpretation in this case as v above. Then $qE\{(Y - p)^+\} = c$, that is, $qT_F(p) = c$ so that p is a well-defined number between u and v (see above, *A1P4*, *A2P6*, and *A2P4*). For $q=1$ the three numbers u, p and v coincide. Furthermore, suppose the lottery is such that the value of its least valuable prize is actually p (or more), that is, $F(p-) = 0$. Then $u_1 = qE\{Y^+\} - c = q(p + T_F(p)) - c =$ $= qp$ and by *(6)* $u_2 = q(u_1 + T_F(u_1)) - c = q(qp + T_F(qp)) - c$. But $T_F(qp) = T_F(p) + p(1 - q)$ since $F(p-) = 0$. Thus, $u_2 = q(p + T_F(p)) -$ $- c = qp = u_1$ etc. Hence, $u_j = qp$ for $j \geqq 1$, by mathematical induction.

Suppose instead that the least valuable prize of the lottery has the value u (or more). This is a weaker condition than the one above, since $u < p$, and the same argument yields the result $u_j = u$ for $j \geqq 1$, which is a mere substitution of u:s for v:s in the corresponding result of Section 2.4. To see the relation between p and u, it is to be noted that the harder condition of the preceding paragraph implies that $qp = u$. This is easily confirmed by checking *(9)* which defines u uniquely. Thus, for $T_F(p-) = 0$, *(9)* may be written as $u = q(u + p - u + T_F(p)) - c \equiv qp$. Then, in this case, u is simply the present value of p, occuring one period hence. Otherwise u is less than qp; the probability of getting something less than p in the next observation is positive if $F(p-) \neq 0$ (see 4.3.3).

Suppose again that $F(u-) = 0$. This case also sheds some light on the equation by which u is defined; if you have observed u, you are then indifferent to stopping or making just one more observation before stopping. Let us elaborate this.

If you continue, you are sure to get at least u again but one period later. The total cost of continuing will then be the sum of the cost of the observation plus the foregone alternative revenue (interest) on what you would have had by stopping now, that is $c + urq$. The q in the last term is there since the interest is not due until the next period.

On the revenue side you will get an improvement of $\max(Y - u, 0)$ on what you have, the expected value of which is $T_F(u)$. Since this is not due until the next period, it must be discounted to be commensurable to the above cost. Thus, u must satisfy the equation

$$(10) \qquad qT_F(u) = c + urq$$

which is equivalent to *(9)* (note that $rq \equiv 1 - q$) and by which u is determined uniquely (*A2P3*). Dividing both members by q (multiplying by $1 + r$) yields

$$(11) \qquad T_F(u) = c(1 + r) + ur$$

where all relevant consequences are discounted to the next period. This formulation is convenient when it comes to a comparison between u, p and v (see 4.3.3 below).

All remaining interpretations in Section 4.4 regarding v_j and v have obvious counterparts for u_j and u. Thus, in essence the introduction of discounting into the basic model (without recall) amounts to a contraction of the optimal levels of aspiration.

4.3.3 The numbers u, p, and v. In conclusion a graphical illustration of the relations between the numbers u, p, and v will be given. They are defined by the equations

$(12) \qquad T_F(v) = c$ by *A2D1*, *(9)* for $q=1$ or *(11)* for $r=0$

$(13) \qquad T_F(p) = c(1 + r)$ $qE\{(Y-p)^+\} = c$, see 4.3.2

$(14) \qquad T_F(u) = c(1 + r) + ur$ *(11)* again

It is seen that they are equal if $r = 0$. Moreover, since $F(v) < 1$, it follows from *A1P4* that $u < p < v$ if u and r are both of them positive.

Geometrically, $T_F(s)$ stands for the area between $y = 1$ and the curve $y = F(t)$ and to the right of $t = s$ (see A1.1) which gives Figure 2. Only the case $u > 0$ is illustrated. The same technique can be used to illustrate all other cases as well.

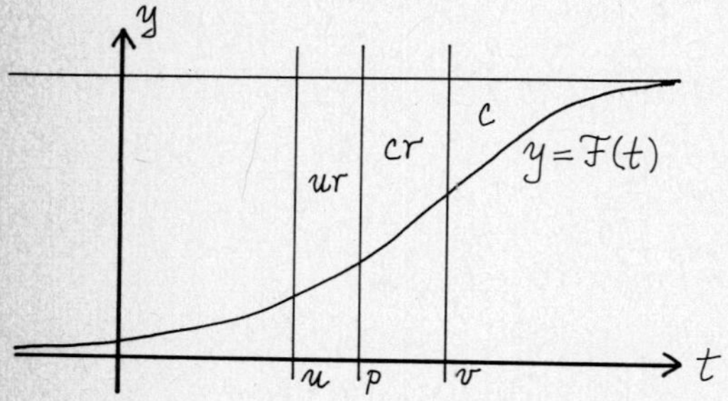

Figure 2 *The numbers u, p, and v in relation to F, c, and r (in principle)*

It can be seen that $p - u > ur$, that is, $u < qp$, unless $F(p-) = 0$. By drawing the curve $y = T_F(s)$ instead of $y = F(t)$ the same information can be conveyed as in Figure 2. This is done in Figure 3. However, here it is possible to see how u can be determined and why it is uniquely determined by *(14)*; $T_F(s)$ is a strictly decreasing (at least for $s < v$) and $c(1 + r) + rs$ is a strictly increasing linear function of s; they are both continuous.

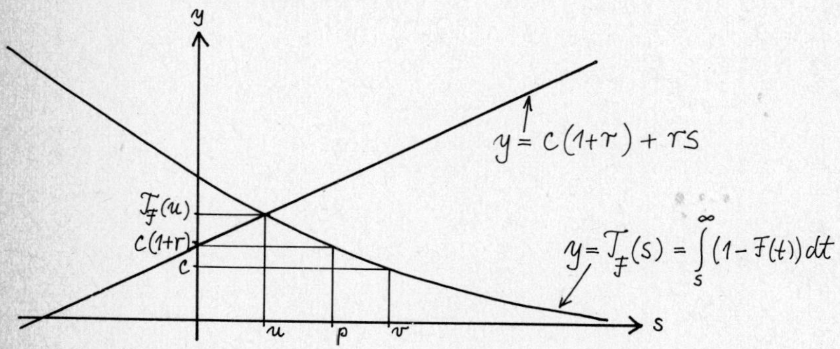

Figure 3 *The numbers u, p, and v in relation to T_F, c, and r (in principle)*

4.4 THE BASIC MODEL WITH RECALL

4.4.1 Basic results. In a process with recall the situation can be described as in Figure 1.

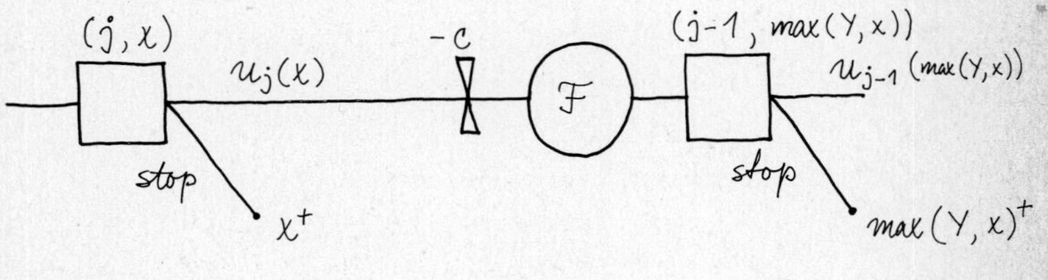

Figure 1 *A decision tree for a process with recall*

From left to right: When you are in (j,x), you have the choice of either stopping, which gives x^+, or continuing, the expected net present value of which is denoted by $u_j(x)$ (the analogue of $v_j(x)$ of Chapter 3), supposing that you follow an optimal decision rule. Then the value to you of being in (j,x) may be written as (see *(4.2.1)* and *(3.3.5)*)

$$(1) \qquad U(j,x) = \max[x^+, u_j(x)]$$

If you choose to continue, you have to pay c at once. Then chance takes over (distribution function F) and sends you to state $(j-1, \max(Y,x))$ where you arrive one period later. Thus $u_j(x)$ can be written as (see *(3.3.4)*)

$$(2) \qquad u_j(x) = -c + qE\{U(j-1, \max(Y,x))\}$$

which by *(1)* or straight from Figure 1 can be written as (see *(3.3.6)*)

$$(3) \qquad u_j(x) = -c + qE\{\max[\max(Y,x)^+, u_{j-1}(\max(Y,x))]\}$$

In order to make *(3)* hold for $j = 1$ as well, it is convenient to define (formally) $u_0(x)$ to be equal to x^+. Then *(3)* can be written

$$(4)\qquad \begin{cases} u_j(x) = qE\{\max[u_0(\max(Y,x)),\ u_{j-1}(\max(Y,x))]\} - c & j \geqq 1 \\ u_0(x) = x^+ \end{cases}$$

which reduces to *(3.3.8)* for $q = 1$ as it ought to do.

The sequence of functions $u_j(x)$ is defined recursively by *(4)*. However, by the same argument as that of Section 5.4, the explicit expression for $u_j(x)$, $j \geqq 1$, can be shown to be (for a proof, see *A4P1*)

$$(5)\qquad u_j(x) = \begin{cases} q^j[x^+ + T_{F^j}(x^+) - T_{F^j}(u)] + u(1 - q^j) & x^+ \leqq u \\ q[x^+ + T_F(x^+) - T_F(u)] + u(1 - q) & x^+ > u \end{cases}$$

where u is uniquely defined by (see *A2D2* and *A2P3*)

$$(6)\qquad qT_F(u) = c + u(1 - q)$$

Thus, u is the same as in the preceding section (see *(4.3.9)*) and for $q = 1$, *(5)* is equivalent to *(3.4.19)*, that is, $u_j(x) \equiv v_j(x)$ as is to be expected. Most properties of $u_j(x)$ are the same, <u>mutatis mutandis</u>, as those of $v_j(x)$. Thus, the equivalences *(5.4.29)* and *(5.4.30)* become (*A4P9*)

$$(7)\qquad u > \max(x^+,\ u_1\ (x)) \Longleftrightarrow u > u_{j+1}(x) > u_j(x) \wedge \lim_{j\to\infty} u_j(x) = u$$

$$(8)\qquad u \leqq \max(x^+,\ u_1(x)) \Longleftrightarrow u_j(x) \equiv u_1(x)$$

in analogy to *(4.3.7)* and *(4.3.8)*. For any fixed value of x, then, the sequence of numbers $u_j(x)$ has the same properties of monotonicity and convergence as u_j of the previous section. Furthermore, if follows from *(5)* that $u_j(x) - x^+$ always thas the same sign as $u - x^+$, that is,

$$(9)\qquad u_j(x) \gtreqless u_0(x) \Longleftrightarrow x^+ \lesseqgtr u$$

in analogy to *(3.4.20)* (for a proof, see *A4P2*); see also *(3.5.5)* and *(3.5.5a)*, the interpretations of which can be more or less literally transferred to the present case.

Also, for $r > 0$, it can be shown that $u_j(x) \leqq v_j(x)$, $x \in R$, $j \geqq 1$ with strict inequality if $F(0) < 1$ (see *A4P10*). Thus, in essence the introduction of discounting into the basic model <u>with</u> recall amounts to a contraction of the optimal levels of aspiration (just like we found in 4.3.2 for a process <u>without</u> recall).

4.4.2 <u>A more conversational treatment</u>. We shall now derive an optimal decision rule and an explicit expression for $u_j(x)$ by making use of the arguments of 3.6.1 and 3.6.3.

Firstly, you should always continue if the expected present value of the increase in your net gain from making just one more observation is positive. Suppose you are in (j,x), $j \geqq 1$. The expected present value of the increase in your gain due to the next observation is $qE\{\max(Y - x^+, 0)\} = qT_F(x^+)$. The cost of the observation is the sum of c (outlay) and the present value of the return (foregone) on what you would have collected on stopping, that is, $c + qrx^+$. Thus, you should always go on if $T_F(x^+) > c(1 + r) + rx^+$, that is, if $x^+ < u$ (see Figure 4.3.3).

Recall that $u_j(x)$ was defined to be the expected net present value of continuing from state (j,x). Then $u_1(x) - x^+$ must be equal to $qT_F(x^+) - c - qrx^+$, that is, $u_1(x) = q(x^+ + T_F(x^+)) - c$. By use of *(6)* (or *A2D2*) this can be written as

$$(10) \qquad u_1(x) = q[x^+ + T_F(x^+) - T_F(u)] + u(1 - q)$$

which is seen to agree with *(5)*.

Secondly, you should always stop if $x^+ > u$. Making just one more observation is then definitely unfavourable, and making <u>at most</u> two more observations (or any other positive number) will not make things better. Since F and c never change, the expected loss incurred by making the first observation can never be expected to be recovered by later observations. Thus, in a process with recall and discounting (and unchanged F and c) you should follow the decision rule

$$\text{(11)} \qquad \text{If you are in } (j,x),\ j \geqq 1, \text{ then } \begin{cases} \underline{\text{stop}} \text{ if } & \text{if } x^+ > u \\ \underline{\text{continue}} & \text{if } x^+ < u \end{cases}$$

or one that is equivalent to it. Those rules are the only optimal decision rules for this process. See (3.6.1) and the discussion following it on what to do when $x^+ = u$ etc. In the remainder of this section only the rule "<u>stop</u> iff $x^+ > u$" will be examined.

Suppose you are in (j,x), $j \geqq 1$, and decide to follow this rule from the next stage on. If $x^+ > u$ and if you actually continue, the rule will tell you to stop after you have made the next observation, so you will then behave as if j were equal to 1. Hence,

$$\text{(12)} \qquad u_j(x) \equiv u_1(x) \qquad x^+ > u,\ j \geqq 1$$

which, like (10) agrees with (5). Then, what remains to be determined is $u_j(x)$ for $x^+ \leqq u$ and $j > 1$.

Let N denote the number of observations you make before stopping if you follow the rule above, starting in (j,x), where $x^+ \leqq u$ and $j > 1$. You will then make at least one more observation, so N will be a non-negative integer-valued random variable having the probability function (see (3.6.11) and the argument that led to it)

$$\text{(13)} \qquad P\{N = n\} = \begin{cases} F^{n-1}(u)\,(1 - F(u)) & 1 \leqq n \leqq j-1 \\ F^{j-1}(u) & n = 1 \end{cases}$$

The present value of the cost of these observations is $c + cq + \ldots + cq^{N-1} = c(1 - q^N)/(1 - q)$, $q \neq 1$, the expected value of which can be determined by use of *(13)*. It is found to be

$$(14) \qquad E\left\{\sum_{n=1}^{N} cq^{n-1}\right\} = \frac{c}{1-q}(1 - E\{q^N\}) = c\,\frac{1-q^jF^j(u)}{1-qF(u)}.$$

For $q = 1$ we get $cE\{N\}$; see *(3.6.12)*.

Let $q^N R_N$ denote the present value of what you collect if you stop after exactly N observations, using the rule above. Then the net present value of participating in the process, using the decision rule above, is $q^N R_N - \sum_{n=1}^{N} cq^{n-1}$, the expected value of which is equal to $u_j(x)$ by definition. Then, since $E\left\{\sum_{n=1}^{N} cq^{n-1}\right\}$ is known by *(14)*, what remains to be done is to determine $E\{q^N R_N\}$. By substituting u for v, the argument that led to *(3.6.17)* and *(3.6.18)* is applicable here too and gives

$$(15) \qquad E\{R_N | N = n\} = u + \frac{T_F(u)}{1 - F(u)} \qquad 1 \leqq n \leqq j-1$$

and

$$(16) \qquad E\{R_N | N = j\} = u - \frac{1}{F^{j-1}(u)} \int_{x^+}^{u} F^j(t)dt + T_F(u)$$

Noting that $E\{q^N R_N | N = n\} = q^n E\{R_N | N = n\}$, we find that

$$(17) \qquad E\{q^N R_N\} = \sum_{n=1}^{j} E\{q^N R_N | N = n\} P\{N = n\} = \sum_{n=1}^{j} q^n E\{R_N | N = n\} P\{N=n\}$$

which can be determined by making use of *(13)*, *(15)*, and *(16)*. After some algebraic manipulations it can be written in the form

$$(18) \qquad E\{q^N R_N\} = u - q^j \int_{x^+}^{u} F^j(t)dt + c\,\frac{1-q^jF^j(u)}{1-qF(u)}$$

the last term of which is equal to the expected present value of the cost of the observations made (see *(14)*). Hence, $u_j(x)$ can be written as

$$(19) \qquad u_j(x) \doteq u - q^j \int_{x^+}^{u} F^j(t)dt = q^j[x^+ + T_{F^j}(x^+) - T_{F^j}(u)] + u(1-q^j)$$

for $x^+ \leqq u$ and $j > 1$, which is seen to agree with *(5)*.

When taken together, the explicit expression for $u_j(x)$ given by *(10)*, *(12)* and *(19)*, is seen to be the same as the one given by *(5)*. As in the case without discounting, it is thus possible to derive $u_j(x)$ by a more direct argument than that of solving *(4)* by mathematical induction.

4.4.3 An optimal decision rule for an infinite process. For the case of an infinite process, one in which you will never be forced to stop, the argument of Section 3.7 is directly applicable. Thus, an optimal decision rule is to be found among the rules of the form

$$(20) \qquad \underline{\text{stop}}, \text{ iff } x^+ > t \qquad t \geqq 0$$

$$(20') \qquad \underline{\text{stop}}, \text{ iff } x^+ \geqq t \qquad t \geqq 0$$

If the expected present value of your net gain from following a particular one of these rules (for $t = t_0$) cannot be improved upon by following another one of these rules (for some $t \neq t_0$), then there exists an optimal decision rule for the process (namely the one for which $t = t_0$). Only the set of rules defined by *(20)* will be examined here. A similar argument leads to the same conclusion for the set defined by *(20')* (see 3.7).

Then, for $t \geqq 0$ and such that $F(t) < 1$, the argument of 4.4.2 is again applicable. Substituting t for u the counterparts of *(13)*, *(14)*, and *(15)* are, respectively,

$$(21) \qquad P\{N = n\} = F^{n-1}(t)(1 - F(t)) \qquad n \geqq 1$$

(22) $E\left\{\sum_{n=1}^{N} cq^{n-1}\right\} = c/(1 - qF(t))$ cf (3.7.7)

(23) $E\{R_N | N = n\} = t + T_F(t)/(1 - F(t))$ $n \geqq 1$ cf (3.7.6)

which by (17) gives

(24) $$E\{q^N R_N\} = t + \frac{qT_F(t) - t(1 - q)}{1 - qF(t)}$$

For each $t \geqq 0$, let $W(t)$ denote the expected present value of your net gain from following rule (20). Then $W(t) = E\left\{q^N R_N - \sum_{n=1}^{N} cq^{n-1}\right\}$ and by (24) and (22)

(25) $$W(t) = t + \frac{qT_F(t) - t(1 - q) - c}{1 - qF(t)}$$ cf (3.7.8)

Since $c = qT_F(u) - u(1 - q)$ by A2D2, (25) can be rewritten as

(26) $$W(t) = t + q[\int_t^u (1 - F(s))ds + (u - t)(1 - q)]/(1 - qF(t))$$

Suppose $u \geqq 0$. Then $W(u) = u$ and for $t \neq u$

(27) $$W(t) \leqq t + (u - t)[q(1 - F(t)) + 1 - q] / (1 - qF(t)) = u$$

so that

(28) $$W(t) \leqq W(u) \qquad t \geqq 0, u \geqq 0$$

If u is negative, it follows from the argument that led to (11), that you should stop whatever state you are in.

We conclude that the decision rule

(29) <u>stop</u> iff $x^+ > u$ cf (3.7.12)

is an optimal decision rule for the process. Hence, the introduction of discounting into an infinite process of this kind only amounts to a contraction of the optimal level of aspiration, u being substituted for v, (*A2P6*).

4.5 CONCLUSION

It has now been shown that the introduction of discounting into the basic models essentially amounts to a contraction of the optimal levels of aspiration of the "undiscounted" models. Properties of existence of an optimal decision rule (and of the optimality of a myopic decision rule; cf 3.7), properties of monotonicity of the optimal levels of aspiration (in both state variables) and of their convergence as the number of possible observations increases, are all preserved.

We now leave the basic models where F and c are always the same, and turn to the case where the cost of an observation varies as you continue.

5 A Generalization of the Basic Models – Variable Cost per Observation

5.1 INTRODUCTION

In this chapter we shall examine the consequences of dropping the assumption that the cost of each observation is the same. As before, you know the cost of each future observation, they are all positive but they need no longer be equal.

Two special cases will be treated in some detail, including the conditions under which a myopic decision rule is optimal. In one, costs are assumed to increase as you go on while in the other, they are assumed to decrease; in the first case later observations are successively more expensive (resource-consuming) than the first, while in the second case the first observation is the most expensive one whereas later observations are successively less expensive.

It is easy to find situations that have major traits in common with these cases. For example, consider a project for developing a new product (cf 2.5). Each period's delay of the completion may be successively more expensive for various reasons. This is then an example of increasing costs, "gradual forced stopping". On the other hand, consider a drug screening project. Once the first few compounds have been analysed and some skill has been achieved, the remaining ones are relatively easy to examine. This is then a case of decreasing costs.

In Section 5.2 some general comments are made on notation and assumptions and on some conclusions that may be expected to hold. The case of discounting and no recall is treated in Section 5.3, based on the results of 4.3 and of Chapter 2. The material in the remaining sections (except the last one), is independent of that of 5.3.

The next three sections are devoted to the case of recall. The general case without discounting is treated in 5.4, the major part of which is a description of the heuristics involved in the determination of an explicit expression for the optimal level of aspiration (5.4.2). This is an example of how an economic problem can be solved by mathematical intuition when economic intuition fails to provide an answer. The explicit expression is given in 5.4.3. Based on this, corresponding results are derived in Section 5.5 for the two special cases of increasing and decreasing unit cost. As they stand, these results may not seem too obvious from an economic point of view, so conversational arguments for their justification are given as well.

The effects of discounting are studied in Section 5.6, the main result of which is the discovery of a rule by which any expression occurring in the no-discounting case can easily be generalized to its counterpart in the discounting case.

The main results are summarized in Section 5.7.

5.2 ASSUMPTIONS, NOTATION AND SOME GENERAL COMMENTS

For detailed statements of the assumptions, see the corresponding sections of the previous chapters. The only one to be changed is the one saying that the cost of each lottery ticket (observation) is always the same.

The state of the process is still characterized by an ordered pair (j,x), where j stands for the number of periods remaining before you are forced to stop and x stands for the value of the observation that you would collect upon stopping at once unless you prefer to collect nothing. As previously, you know the cost of each future observation. They are all positive but they need no longer be equal. Thus, when in (j,x), you know the (ordered) set of j possibly different, positive numbers, each one of which denotes the cost of a particular one of the remaining possible observations. Then, to be consistent with the numbering of the states, let c_j denote the cost of the next observation, the one made by leaving (j,x) without stopping.

No other changes in notation will be made. Thus, e g $v_j(x)$, when it occurs later in this chapter, has the same meaning as before (see 3.3) except that only the weak assumption above regarding the cost of future observations is understood to hold (and similarly for u_j, and $u_j(x)$; see 4.3 and 4.4) unless something else is stated explicitly.

Two special cases will be treated separately. One is that in which future observations become more and more costly and the other is that in which they become less and less costly. Suppose you are in (j,x). Then in the first case, $0 < c_j < c_{j-1} < \ldots < c_1$, while in the other case, $c_j > c_{j-1} > \ldots > c_1 > 0$.

In the first case, the longer you continue, the more expensive will the next observation be. This case is then fairly similar to the ones treated in the previous chapters. There the cost of an observation was assumed to be <u>constant</u> for a given number of observations and then <u>infinite</u>; when you can no longer continue, the cost of the "next" observation may be regarded as infinite. Here the cost of an observation is assumed to increase all the time (by finite jumps) until you are forced to stop. It then seems reasonable to expect the optimal levels of aspiration to have the same properties of monotonicity in this case as in those of the previous chapters. However, this is an intuitive conclusion. the truth or falsity of which will have to be proved.

In the other case, the longer you continue, the cheaper will the next observation be. Then, even if the first ones are "too expensive" in themselves, it may be worthwhile to make them in order to be able to make the later "cheap" ones. This seems reasonable if you are sufficiently far away from the point of forced stopping (where the cost of continuing suddenly rises to infinity) and if the later observations are "sufficiently cheap" compared to the earlier ones. The details of this argument will have to be worked out.

In the general case, bounds on the optimal levels of aspiration is all that can be given on intuitive grounds (at least if my, the authors, intuition is being used). Suppose you are in (j,x), $j > 1$. Let C_j' denote the most expensive one and c_j' the least expensive one of the future observations, that is, $C_j' = \max_{1 \leqslant k \leqslant j} c_k$ and $c_j' = \min_{1 \leqslant k \leqslant j} c_k$. Then determine the optimal level of aspiration according to the appropriate one of the previous models for $c = C_j'$ and for $c = c_j'$. Let these levels be denoted by A_j and a_j, respectively. Then $C_j' \geqq c_j'$ and $A_j \leqq a_j$. If $x^+ \leqq A_j$ you should continue, since A_j is "too pessimistic" a level of aspiration that does not take into account the fact that later observations may cost less than C_j'. Similarly, if $x^+ > a_j$, you should stop, since a_j is "too optimistic" a level of aspiration that does not take into account the fact that later observations may cost more than c_j'. Thus, in the general case your optimal level of aspiration is a number between A_j and a_j when you are in (j,x). Clearly, if the cost of each future observation is the same, then $C_j' = c_j'$ and $A_j = a_j$ so that one of the previous models is back again.

5.3 DISCOUNTING AND NO RECALL

5.3.1 The general case. Following the argument of section 4.3, the situation can be described as in Figure 1.

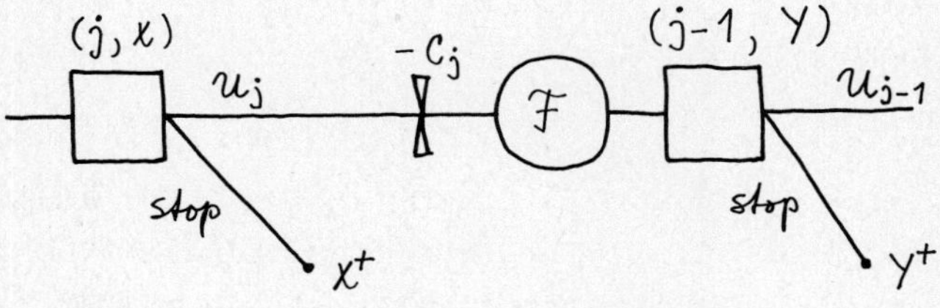

Figure 1 *A decision tree for a process without recall (variable cost)*

In (j,x), $j \geqq 1$, you know the cost of each possible future observation, that is, you know c_k for $1 \leqq k \leqq j$, all of which are positive. If you stop, you get x^+. u_j denotes the expected present value (using a discount factor of q) of your net gain from continuing, provided that you follow an optimal decision rule from the next period onwards. Then (cf (4.3.4)).

$$(1) \qquad u_j = -c_j + qE\{\max(Y^+, u_{j-1})\} \qquad j > 1$$

As before, we make the formal definition $u_0 = 0$ in order to make (1) hold for $j = 1$ as well. Keeping this is mind, the same argument that led to (2.3.5) and (4.3.6) implies that (1) can be rewritten as

$$(2) \qquad u_j = \begin{cases} qT_F(0) - c_j & u_{j-1} \leqq 0 \\ q(u_{j-1} + T_F(u_{j-1})) - c_j & u_{j-1} > 0 \end{cases} \qquad j \geqq 1$$

Pursuing the analogy with the constant-cost case, define the sequence of numbers w_j, $j \geqq 1$, corresponding to u of the constant-cost case, by

$$(3) \qquad w_j = q[w_j + T_F(w_j)] - c_j \qquad j \geqq 1$$

see *(4.3.9)*. From *A2D2* it follows that w_j bears the same relation to q, F and c_j as u does to q, F and c. In particular, we then get

$$(4) \qquad w_j \gtreqless w_k \Leftrightarrow c_j \lesseqgtr c_k \qquad j,k \geqq 1 \qquad (A2P8)$$

$$(5) \qquad w_j \gtreqless 0 \Leftrightarrow qT_F(0) - c_j \gtreqless 0 \qquad j \geqq 1 \qquad (A2P7)$$

which will be referred to frequently in the sequel.

By substituting the expression for c_j given by *(3)* into *(2)* and then using the definition of T_F (*A1D1*) we get

$$(6) \qquad u_j = w_j - q\int_{u_{j-1}^{+}}^{w_j} F(t)dt \qquad j \geqq 1$$

which relates u_j to w_j. For the purpose of studying the properties of monotonicity of u_j, *(6)* is often a more convenient expression to use than *(2)* (see e.g. the proof of *A3P4*).

The only optimal decision rules are seen to be those which tell you to stop if $x^+ > u_j$, and to continue if $x^+ < u_j$, when you are in (j,x), $j \geqq 1$. As before, u_j may then be interpreted as your optimal level of aspiration in (j,x), $j \geqq 1$ (cf 2.4 and 4.3.2). However, without some more restrictive assumption regarding the cost of future observations there is not much more to be said. Therefore, two special cases will be treated below. In one, costs are increasing and in the other they are decreasing.

5.3.2 Increasing unit cost. Here some general properties of the optimal levels of aspiration u_j, will be derived under the more restrictive assumption

$$(7) \qquad c_{j+1} < c_j \qquad j \geqq 1$$

that is, the cost per observation increases as you go on. Remember that the periods are numbered in reverse. It follows from *(4)* that the assumption *(7)* is equivalent to

$$(8) \qquad w_j < w_{j+1} \qquad j \geqq 1$$

Suppose $w_1 \leqq 0$. Then $u_1 = qT_F(0) - c_1 \leqq 0$ by *(2)* and *(5)*, so you should stop at $(1,x)$ if $x > 0$. Moreover, there is no harm in stopping even if $x = 0$, since there is then no advantage to be had from continuing. Thus, you may as well relabel the states (fix your horizon) in such a way that $w_1 > 0$ in the new notation. This is always possible unless all the relevant w_j:s are non-positive, in which case the above argument implies that you may as well refrain from making any observations at all. Hence, the condition

$$(9) \qquad 0 < w_j < w_{j+1} \qquad j \geqq 1$$

is assumed to hold throughout this subsection. It then follows from *(5)* that $qT_F(0) - c_j$ is positive for $j \geqq 1$. This quantity denotes the expected present value of making just one more observation when you are in (j,x), so you should continue if x^+ is less than this. Consequently, only if x^+ is a sufficiently large positive number, should you stop before you have reached your horizon, that is, $u_j > 0$ for $j \geqq 1$.

By definition w_j has the same properties as u (or v) for any fixed j (see *(3)*). Remember that v and u (if positive) could be interpreted as your optimal level of aspiration in a process without forced stopping in the constant-cost case (see 2.4 and 4.3.2). Then w_j (which is positive by *(9)*) denotes the expected net present value of continuing in an infinite process with constant cost per observation equal to c_j whereas u_j stands for the corresponding value in a finite process (no more than j observations) where the cheapest observation costs c_j. Hence, $w_j \geqq u_j$, $j \geqq 1$. Furthermore, if you are sure to get at least w_j in each observation, then $w_j = u_j$; if you are not, then the infinite process is the more advantageous one, so $w_j > u_j$. Thus, using *(6)*, $w_j = u_j$ iff $F(w_j-) = 0$.

By a similar argument we may conclude that $u_{j+1} > u_j$, $j \geqq 1$. When you are in $(j+1, x)$, the next j observations are all of them (one by one) cheaper than the corresponding ones if you are in (j,x). However, the prospective gain is the same, and on top of it you may continue for one more period (and $u_1 > 0$ so you may actually wish to exploit this opportunity).

It follows from *(9)* that $F(w_j-) > 0 \Rightarrow F(w_{j+n}-) > 0$, $n \geqq 0$, and $F(w_j-) = 0 \Rightarrow F(w_{j-n}) = 0$, $0 \leqq n \leqq j-1$ so the above argument leads to the conclusions

$$(11) \qquad F(w_j-) = 0 \Rightarrow w_{j-n} = u_{j-n} > u_{j-n-1} \qquad 0 \leqq n \leqq j-1$$

$$(12) \qquad F(w_1-) > 0 \Rightarrow w_{j+1} > u_{j+1} > u_j \qquad j \geqq 0$$

Let us examine *(11)*. Suppose you are in (j,x), $j \geqq 1$, and suppose that $F(w_j-) = 0$. If (j,x) is your initial state, then $x = 0$. Otherwise you have already made an observation the value of which is at least w_j, that is, $x^+ = x \geqq w_j$. In either case you should make at the most one more observation; you will then get at least w_j again, and since $w_j > u_{j-1}$, you should stop there. Thus, you should behave as if you had only one more observation at your disposal. You may then as well relabel the states (fix your horizon) in such a way that $F(w_2-) > 0$ in the new notation, for then $F(w_j-) = 0$ only if $j = 1$, and in any case that is how you should behave.

When all this relabelling has been done, you will have fixed your horizon in such a way that

$$(13) \qquad w_1 > 0 \wedge F(w_2-) > 0$$

and if this cannot be done, you should either stop where you are or make just one more observation, no matter what state you happen to be in. We shall therefore assume *(13)* to hold (in addition to *(8)*). We have then assumed away all trivial processes, trivial in the sense that you know from the outset that you will not make more than one observation; you are then facing just <u>one</u> decision, not a sequence of decisions.

By *(11)* and *(12)*, *(8)*, and *(13)* are seen to imply

$$(14) \qquad w_{j+1} > u_{j+1} > u_j > 0 \qquad j \geqq 1$$

so that the direction of change of your optimal level of aspiration is the same as in the constant-cost case (see *(4.3.7)*). A mathematical argument that leads to the same conclusions can be modelled on the proofs of A3 with *(3)* and *(6)* as starting points.

You will also see that no myopic decision rule is optimal. Such a rule will tell you to use $qT_F(0) - c_j$ for level of aspiration when you are in (j,x), whereas the optimal level of aspiration is u_j. However, $u_j > qT_F(0) - c_j > 0$ for $j \geqq 2$, by *(14)* and *(2)*, so the myopic decision rule may tell you to stop too soon.

5.3.3 <u>Decreasing unit cost</u>. Here the sequence of numbers u_j, $j \geqq 1$, will be studied under the assumption

$$(15) \qquad c_{j+1} > c_j \qquad j \geqq 1$$

that is, the cost per observation is assumed to decrease as you go on. We shall proceed in the manner of 5.3.2 with the aim of finding out whether a myopic decision rule can ever be equivalent to an optimal decision rule, except in trivial cases. Thus, we start by excluding those cases about which you know from the outset that you should not make more than one observation (one or zero), no matter what state you happen to be in. Such a process will be called an <u>inessential process</u>.

By a <u>process</u> we simply mean a lottery and the rules of it (see 2.1). (More formally, a process may be <u>defined</u> as a quadruple (F, j, x, c_k), where F has the same meaning as before, (j,x) is your starting state, and c_k stands for the whole sequence of costs, c_k, $1 \leqq k \leqq j$. Whenever this formalism is being used, it will be clear from the context what other conditions are assumed to hold, e.g. here we treat processes with discounting, no recall, and such that *(15)* holds.)

It follows from *(4)* that the assumption *(15)* is equivalent to

(16) $$w_{j+1} < w_j \qquad j \geqq 1$$

so we may as well exclude those processes for which $w_1 \leqq 0$ or $F(w_1-) = 0$, since they are clearly inessential. The remaining ones satisfy the condition

(17) $$w_1 > 0 \text{ and } F(w_1-) > 0$$

which, by *(6)*, is equivalent to

(18) $$w_1 > u_1 > 0$$

Obviously, we need only consider processes in which you can make at the least two observations. Moreover, since later observations are cheaper, if there is to be at least one state from which it may be advantageous to continue for more than one period, then one of those states must be $(2,x)$ for some x, the two last observations (costing c_2 and c_1) being the cheapest. We may then exclude those processes for which u_2 is either non-positive or undefined.

Now where are we? Our aim is to determine whether an optimal decision rule for this process (given *(15)*) can ever be a myopic rule. As before, two decision rules are said to be equivalent iff whatever state you are in, one rule will tell you to do the same thing as the other. In this case a myopic rule is one that is equivalent to

(19) If you are in (j,x), $j \geqq 1$, then $\begin{array}{ll} \underline{\text{stop}} & \text{if } x^+ > qT_F(0) - c_j \\ \underline{\text{continue}} & \text{if } x^+ < qT_F(0) - c_j \end{array}$

that is, following a myopic rule means acting as if the next observation were to be the last one, no matter what state you are in.

So far we have shown that the only processes of this kind (obeying *(15)*) in which there may be a state from which it will be advantageous to continue for more than one period, are those which satisfy the condition

$$(20) \qquad w_1 > u_1 > 0 \text{ and } u_2 > 0$$

All other processes (satisfying *(15)* but <u>not</u> *(20)*) are inessential. Hence, the sequential nature of these processes is only spurious, and we can exclude them from further discussion.

In the general case, the optimal level of aspiration is u_j at (j,x), $j \geqq 1$. Let u'_j denote the corresponding myopic level of aspiration, that is,

$$(21) \qquad u'_j = qT_F(0) - c_j = \int_0^{w_j}(1 - qF(t))dt \qquad j \geqq 1$$

by *(19)* and *(3)*. If $u'_j = u_j$ for $j \geqq 2$ the two decision rules are clearly equivalent. However, if, for some j, u'_j and u_j are both of them non-positive (and possibly different), then either rule may tell you to stop, so the weaker condition

$$(22) \qquad u'_j = u_j \qquad j \in \{k | k \geqq 2 \wedge \max(u'_k, u_k) > 0\}$$

is sufficient for a myopic decision rule to be optimal.

Consider now those processes which satisfy both *(15)* and *(20)*. Does one of those satisfy *(22)* as well? [We note in passing that (by *(17)* and *(24)*) the sign of u'_j is then always the same as that of w_j (cf *A2P4* and the discussion of v and v_1 in 2.4).] For such a process u_j may be positive even if u'_j is negative since future observations are always cheaper than the next one; if you behave in a myopic way, you will certainly not overestimate what the future has to offer. Hence $u_j \geqq u'_j$, and *(22)* may then be rewritten as

(23) $u'_j = u_j \qquad j \in \{k \mid k \geqq 2 \wedge u_k > 0\}$

If $u_k \leqq 0$, then you may as well stop at (k,x). Moreover, since the observations that you may have to make before arriving there are even more expensive than those available to you afterwards, it will seem reasonable that

(24) $u_k \leqq 0 \Rightarrow u_{k+n+1} < u_{k+n} \leqq 0 \qquad n \geqq 0,\ k \geqq 1$

This may also be shown by (6). Let m be the largest integer such that $u_m > 0$. Then $m \geqq 2$ by (20) and $u_k > 0$ for each k such that $2 \leqq k \leqq m$. Hence, (23) may be rewritten as

(25) $u'_j = u_j \qquad 2 \leqq j \leqq m$

For $2 \leqq j \leqq m$ (6) may be reformulated as

(26) $u_j = \int_0^{w_j}(1 - qF(t))dt + \int_0^{u_{j-1}} qF(t)dt$

since u_{j-1} is then positive. Hence, by (21)

(27) $u_j - u'_j = \int_0^{u_{j-1}} qF(t)dt \qquad 2 \leqq j \leqq m$

which is seen to be non-negative as was to be expected.

Consider the case $j = 2$. Then by (27), (6), and (20),

(26) $u_2 - u'_2 = \int_0^{u_1} qF(t)dt = \int_{u_1}^{w_1}(1 - qF(t))dt > 0$

Thus, (25) does not hold; if you are in $(2,x)$, where $u'_2 < x^+ < u_2$, you will be told to stop by a myopic rule whereas an optimal rule will tell you to go on.

But (25) ((22)) is only a sufficient condition for a myopic rule to be optimal. If the process is such that you will never observe a value x, such that $u'_j < x^+ < u_j$ for some $2 \leqq j \leqq m$, you may as well follow the myopic decision rule. In the above case, if (and only if), F is such that $F(u_2-) - F(u_2') = 0$, the two rules will always (with probability one) tell you to do the same thing when only two observations remain.

In conclusion: If $c_{j+1} > c_j$, $j \geqq 1$, then no myopic decision rule is optimal for a process where $F(u_2-) > F(u_2')$ (unless the process is inessential).

We refrain from developing the argument any further. Please consider it as a starting point for further investigations regarding the conditions for optimality of myopic decision rules.

5.4 RECALL - THE GENERAL CASE

5.4.1 The recursive relation. Following the argument of section 6.4, the situation can be described as in Figure 1.

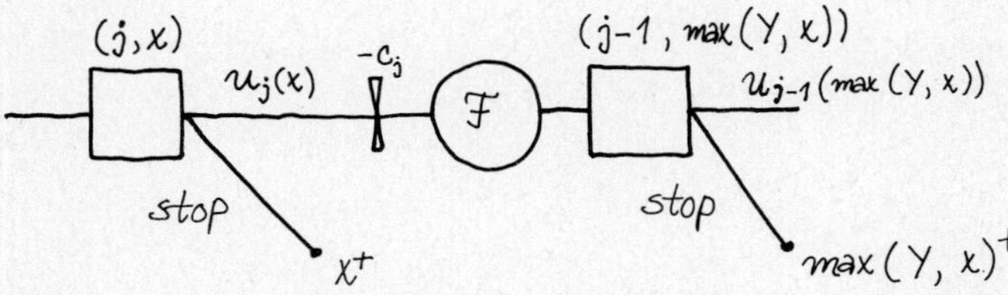

Figure 1 *A decision tree for a process with recall (variable cost)*

In (j,x), $j \geqq 1$, you know the cost of each possible future observation, that is, you know c_k for $1 \leqq k \leqq j$, all of which are positive. If you stop, you get x^+. $u_j(x)$ denotes the expected present value (using a discount factor of q) of your net gain from continuing, provided that you follow an optimal decision rule from the next period onwards. If you continue, you are taken to state $(j - 1, \max(Y,x))$ since earlier observations may be recalled. Then (see (4.4.3))

$$(1) \qquad u_j(x) = -c_j + qE\{\max[\max(Y,x)^+,\ u_{j-1}(\max(Y,x))]\} \qquad j > 1$$

As before we make the formal definition $u_0(x) = x^+$ in order to make *(1)* hold for $j = 1$ as well. Keeping this in mind, $u_j(x)$ is uniquely determined by *(1)*.

Now the problem has been translated into mathematics. Here it seems pointless (to me) to attempt to derive an explicit expression for $u_j(x)$ by the "direct" arguments of 3.5, say. However, as in 3.4, an argument by mathematical induction may work. The main trouble then consists of finding a sensible assumption on which to base the proof, for once a good assumption has been found, it is a comparatively easy task to show whether it is correct or not (see A5).

Therefore, the next subsection is devoted to a detailed report of how I found one, It is included here as an example of the heuristics involved in this kind of problem-solving. However, there is no loss in continuity by going straight to 5.4.3 where the explicit expression for $u_j(x)$ is given.

So as to make the notation as simple as possible, only the case of no discounting $(q = 1)$ will be treated. Based on the experience gained here, the case with discounting will be treated in Section 5.6.

5.4.2 An outline of a derivation. Consider the sequence of functions v_j, $j \geqq 1$, defined recursively by

$$(1') \qquad \begin{cases} v_j(x) = -c_j + E\{\max[\max(Y,x)^+,\ v_{j-1}(\max(Y,x))]\} \\ v_0(x) = x^+,\ c_j > 0 \end{cases} \qquad j \geqq 1$$

which is the same as *(1)* above for $q = 1$. Our aim is to find an explicit expression for $v_j(x)$ by mathematical induction. Then the first thing to be done is to find out enough about the structure of $v_j(x)$ to dare to attempt a guess at what this expression will look like. The procedure to be used for this "generation of hypotheses" will be the same as in section 3.4, namely to derive $v_j(x)$ explicitly from *(1')* for $j = 1, 2, \ldots$ for as many values of j as seems necessary to make a reasonable guess at the general expression. In fact, this procedure generates a very real optimal stopping problem, unfortunately one of a more general nature than those treated here.

The next thing to be done is to see if the guess is correct, to test the hypothesis. The test consists of showing that if the guess is correct for some value of j, then it is also correct for $j + 1$. If this can be done, then the guess was correct and the aim has been achieved. If the opposite can be shown, then the guess was wrong and we shall either have to find a better one or abandon the whole idea.

This report is an outline of my original preliminary manuscript, only leaving out some lengthy but elementary algebraic manipulations. However, no stream-lining has been made, since the main problem of finding a "good guess" appeared to consist of finding an appropriate notation so that the structure is made apparent. The report shows the way I came to use in arriving at such a notation (and I do not claim that it is the "best" way). It is only to be seen as an example of how an economic problem can be solved by "mathematical intuition" when "economic intuition" is insufficient.

Thus consider the sequence of functions defined by *(1')*. Define the sequence of real numbers w'_j, $j \geqq 1$, by (cf *A2D1*)

$$(2) \qquad T_F(w'_j) = c_j \qquad j \geqq 1$$

Then $v_1(x)$ and $v_2(x)$ can be derived directly from *(1')* by entirely elementary manipulations. We get

$$(3) \qquad v_1(x) = x^+ + T_F(x^+) - c_1$$

$$(4) \qquad v_2(x) = \begin{cases} x^+ + T_F(x^+) - c_2 & x^+ > w'_1 \\ x^+ + T_{F^2}(x^+) - c_2 - (T_{F^2}(w'_1) - T_F(w'_1)) & x^+ \leqq w'_1 \end{cases}$$

These derivations (and the ones to follow) proceed by rewriting *(1')* as (see *(3.4.3)*)

$$(5) \qquad v_{j+1}(x) = -c_{j+1} + E\{\max(Y,x)^+\} + + E\{\max[v_j(\max(Y,x)) - \max(Y,x)^+, 0]\}$$

where $E\{\max(Y,x)^+\} = x^+ + T_F(x^+)$ by *A1P1 (iii)* so that

$$(6) \qquad v_{j+1}(x) - x^+ = T_F(x^+) - c_{j+1} + + E\{\max[v_j(\max(Y,x)) - \max(Y,x)^+, 0]\}$$

Now consider $v_3(x)$. For $x^+ > w_1'$, the expression for $v_2(\max(Y,x)) - - \max(Y,x)^+$ given by *(4)*, will produce two branches of $v_3(x)$ when inserted into *(6)*, just like $v_1(x)$ gave rise to the two branches of $v_2(x)$. For $v_3(x)$, one branch will hold for $x^+ > w_1' \wedge x^+ > w_2'$ and another one for $x^+ > w_1' \wedge x^+ \leqq w_2'$. The "dividing point" is that value of x for which $v_2(x) - x^+ = 0$, which plays a critical role in the development of the expected value in the right-hand side of *(6)*.

So, there should be a similar "dividing point" when the case $x^+ \leqq w_1'$ of $v_2(x)$ is treated. Define a_2 by

$$(7) \qquad T_{F^2}(a_2) = c_2 + T_{F^2}(w_1') - T_F(w_1')$$

Evidently $v_2(x) - x^+ = 0$ if $x^+ = a_2$ and $x^+ \leqq w_1'$ (see *(4)*). Moreover, a_2 is uniquely defined by *(7)* since the right-hand side of *(7)* is positive (see *A2P1*). Then two more branches of $v_3(x)$ will be produced, one for $x^+ \leqq w_1' \wedge x^+ > a_2$ and another for $x^+ \leqq w_1' \wedge x^+ \leqq a_2$. What will happen? Is $v_j(x)$ going to have 2^{j-1} branches?

The answer looks like "no"; two of the four branches of $v_3(x)$ turn out to be the same expression, and $v_3(x)$ can be written

$$v_3(x) = \begin{cases} x^+ + T_F(x^+) - c_3 & A \\ x^+ + T_{F^2}(x^+) - c_3 - (T_{F^2}(w_2') - T_F(w_2')) & B \\ x^+ + T_{F^3}(x^+) - c_3 - (T_{F^3}(a_2) - T_F(a_2)) & C \end{cases} \tag{8}$$

$$A = \{x | \max(w_1', w_2') < x^+ \vee a_2 < x^+ \leqq w_1'\}$$

$$B = \{x | w_1' < x^+ \leqq w_2'\}$$

$$C = \{x | x^+ \leqq \min(w_1', a_2)\}$$

However, the question is still not settled. A fair guess would be that $v_j(x)$ contain j branches, but their respective domains may be quite complicated.

So, off we go again. What will $v_4(x)$ look like? The "zeros" of the three branches of $v_3(x) - x^+$ are (see *(8)*)

(9)

A:	w_3'	see *(2)*
B:	b_3	to be defined from *(8)*, see *(7)*
C:	a_3	to be defined from *(8)*, see *(7)*

and we get (from *(8)*, *(9)* and *(1')* after lengthy but routine calculations)

$$v_4(x) - x^+ = \begin{cases} T_F(x^+) - c_4 & A' \\ T_{F^2}(x^+) - c_4 - (T_{F^2}(w_3') - T_F(w_3')) & B' \\ T_{F^3}(x^+) - c_4 - (T_{F^3}(b_3) - T_F(b_3)) & C' \\ T_{F^4}(x^+) - c_4 - (T_{F^4}(a_3) - T_F(a_3)) & D' \end{cases} \tag{10}$$

$$A' = (A \cap \{w_3' < x^+\}) \cup (B \cap \{b_3 < x^+\}) \cup (C \cap \{a_3 < x^+\})$$

$$B' = A \cap \{w_3' \geqq x^+\}$$

$$C' = B \cap \{b_3 \geqq x^+\}$$

$$D' = C \cap \{a_3 \geqq x^+\}$$

This is beginning to look coherent!

Let us rewrite the expressions obtained so far and make use of the definitions of w'_j, a_2, and b_3 ((2), (7), and (9)):

$$\begin{aligned} &w'_j: \quad T_F(w'_j) = c_j \\ &a_2: \quad T_{F^2}(a_2) = c_2 + T_{F^2}(w'_1) - T_F(w'_1) \\ (11) \qquad &a_3: \quad T_{F^3}(a_3) = c_3 + T_{F^3}(a_2) - T_F(a_2) \\ &b_3: \quad T_{F^2}(b_3) = c_3 + T_{F^2}(w'_2) - T_F(w'_2) \end{aligned}$$

We then get (from (11), (3), (4), and (10))

$$v_1(x) - x^+ = T_F(x^+) - T_F(w'_1) \qquad A_1$$

$$v_2(x) - x^+ = \begin{cases} T_F(x^+) - T_F(w'_2) & A_2 \\ T_{F^2}(x^+) - T_{F^2}(a_2) & B_2 \end{cases}$$

$$(12) \qquad v_3(x) - x^+ = \begin{cases} T_F(x^+) - T_F(w'_3) & A_3 \\ T_{F^2}(x^+) - T_{F^2}(b_3) & B_3 \\ T_{F^3}(x^+) - T_{F^3}(a_3) & C_3 \end{cases}$$

$$v_4(x) - x^+ = \begin{cases} T_F(x^+) - T_F(w'_4) & A_4 \\ T_{F^2}(x^+) - T_{F^2}(\quad) & B_4 \\ T_{F^3}(x^+) - T_{F^3}(\quad) & C_4 \\ T_{F^4}(x^+) - T_{F^4}(a_4) & D_4 \end{cases}$$

where subscripts instead of primes are used in the symbols for the domains of the various branches. The blanks within the parentheses in the B_4- and C_4-branches of $v_4(x) - x^+$ will contain b_4 (derived from b_3 like a_3 was derived from a_2; see (11)) and d_4 (which is the first element of a new sequence of constants). It is not yet apparent which one is going where, however. The a_4 in the last branch is an informed guess (look at the last branches of the expressions for the other

$v_j(x)$:s in *(12)*). It should be derived from a_3 like a_3 was derived from a_2; see *(11)*.

Take a good look at *(12)*!

At this point it occurred to me that it would be impractical to keep on using the letters of the alphabet to denote the domains of the respective branches. Here is a case for double subscripts if ever there was one! So, let

$A_1 = D_{11}$	$A_2 = D_{21}$	$A_3 = D_{31}$	$A_4 = D_{41}$
	$B_2 = D_{22}$	$B_3 = D_{32}$	$B_4 = D_{42}$
		$C_3 = D_{33}$	$C_4 = D_{43}$
			$D_4 = D_{44}$

etc., where $D_{11} = R$, the whole real line. By the "etc." it is meant that the k:th branch of $v_j(x)$, the one that is expressed in terms of T_F^k, $1 \leqq k \leqq j$, has D_{jk} as its domain of definition.

Now, $D_{11} = \{x|v_1(x) - x^+ \geqq 0\} \cup \{x|v_1(x) - x^+ < 0\} =$
$= \{x|w_1' \geqq x^+\} \cup \{x|w_1' < x^+\}$ and these two sets are disjoint. Denote them by $D_{11}^{\geqslant}$ and $D_{11}^{<}$, respectively. Then, by *(4)*, $D_{21} = D_{11}^{<}$ and $D_{22} = D_{11}^{\geqslant}$. Similarly D_{21} can be split up into the two disjoint (sub-)sets $D_{21}^{\geqslant} = \{x|x \in D_{21} \wedge v_2(x) - x^+ \geqq 0\}$ and $D_{21}^{<} = \{x|x \in D_{21} \wedge v_2(x) - x^+ < 0\}$. By *(4)*, *(2)*, and *(7)* they can be rewritten as $D_{21}^{\geqslant} = D_{21} \cap \{x|w_2' \geqq x^+\}$ and $D_{21}^{<} = D_{21} \cap \{x|w_2' < x^+\}$. In the same way D_{22} can be partitioned into $D_{22}^{\geqslant} = D_{22} \cap \{x|a_2 \geqq x^+\}$ and $D_{22}^{<} = D_{22} \cap \{x|a_2 < x^+\}$.

Taking a look at *(8)* and putting things together discloses that

$$D_{31} = D_{21}^{<} \cup D_{22}^{<}$$
$$D_{32} = D_{21}^{\geqslant}$$
$$D_{33} = D_{22}^{\geqslant}$$

and, if these sets are partitioned in the same way, it follows from *(10)* that

$D_{41} = D_{31}^{<} \cup D_{32}^{<} \cup D_{33}^{<}$

$D_{42} = D_{31}^{\geq}$

$D_{43} = D_{32}^{\geq}$

$D_{44} = D_{33}^{\geq}$

A possible generalization of this would be

$$D_{j+1\,1} = \bigcup_{k=1}^{j} D_{jk}^{<}$$

$$j \geq 1$$

$$D_{j+1\,k+1} = D_{jk}^{\geq} \qquad 1 \leq k \leq j$$

(13) $$D_{11} = R$$

where $D_{jk}^{\geq} = D_{jk} \cap \{x | v_j(x) - x^+ \geq 0\}$

and $D_{jk}^{<} = D_{jk} \cap \{x | v_j(x) - x^+ < 0\}$

Then $D_{jk} = D_{jk}^{\geq} \cup D_{jk}^{<}$ and $D_{jk}^{\geq} \cap D_{jk}^{<} = \emptyset$ and $\bigcup_{k=1}^{j+1} D_{j+1\,k} = \bigcup_{k=1}^{j} D_{jk}$ for $j \geq 1$. But for $j = 1$, $\bigcup_{k=1}^{j} D_{jk} = D_{11} = R$, so the same must be true for any $j \geq 1$. Thus, the sets D_{jk}, $1 \leq k \leq j$, form a partition of the real line for any value of $j \geq 1$. This adds to the plausibility of *(13)* (which is still only a guess), for $v_j(x)$ will then be uniquely defined for any (j,x).

Now it is tempting to introduce a double subscript notation for the various sequences of constants, $w!$, $a.$, $b.$, as well. It looks as if one such sequence will have to be started in each step from $v_j(x)$ to $v_{j+1}(x)$; see *(12)*. In analogy to D_{jk}, a possible notation would be

$$w_1' = a_{11} \quad w_2' = a_{21} \quad w_3' = a_{31}$$
$$a_2 = a_{22} \quad b_3 = a_{32} \quad \text{etc.}$$
$$a_3 = b_{33}$$

Making use of the new notation, *(12)* can be rewritten as

$$v_1(x) - x^+ = T_F(x^+) - T_F(a_{11}) \qquad D_{11}$$

$$v_2(x) - x^+ = \begin{cases} T_F(x^+) - T_F(a_{21}) & D_{21} \\ T_{F^2}(x^+) - T_{F^2}(a_{22}) & D_{22} \end{cases}$$

$$(14) \qquad v_3(x) - x^+ = \begin{cases} T_F(x^+) - T_F(a_{31}) & D_{31} \\ T_{F^2}(x^+) - T_{F^2}(a_{32}) & D_{32} \\ T_{F^3}(x^+) - T_{F^3}(a_{33}) & D_{33} \end{cases}$$

$$v_4(x) - x^+ = \begin{cases} T_F(x^+) - T_F(a_{41}) & D_{41} \\ T_{F^2}(x^+) - T_{F^2}(a_{42}) & D_{42} \\ T_{F^3}(x^+) - T_{F^3}(a_{43}) & D_{43} \\ T_{F^4}(x^+) - T_{F^4}(a_{44}) & D_{44} \end{cases}$$

where, by rewriting *(11)* and checking *(10)*,

$$(15) \qquad \left.\begin{array}{ll} a_{j1}: & T_F(a_{j1}) = c_j \\ a_{22}: & T_{F^2}(a_{22}) = c_2 + T_{F^2}(a_{11}) - T_F(a_{11}) \\ a_{33}: & T_{F^3}(a_{33}) = c_3 + T_{F^3}(a_{22}) - T_F(a_{22}) \\ a_{32}: & T_{F^2}(a_{32}) = c_3 + T_{F^2}(a_{21}) - T_F(a_{21}) \end{array}\right\} \text{from } (11)$$
$$\left.\begin{array}{ll} a_{44}: & T_{F^4}(a_{44}) = c_4 + T_{F^4}(a_{33}) - T_F(a_{33}) \\ a_{43}: & T_{F^3}(a_{43}) = c_4 + T_{F^3}(a_{32}) - T_F(a_{32}) \\ a_{42}: & T_{F^2}(a_{42}) = c_4 + T_{F^2}(a_{31}) - T_F(a_{31}) \end{array}\right\} \text{from } (10)$$

From *(15)* it can be seen that

$T_{F^j}(a_{jj}) = c_j + T_{F^j}(a_{j-1\ j-1}) - T_F(a_{j-1\ j-1})$

at least for $1 \leqq j \leqq 4$, and that

$T_{F^{j-1}}(a_{j\ j-1}) = c_j + T_{F^{j-1}}(a_{j-1\ j-2}) - T_F(a_{j-1\ j-2})$

at least for $2 \leqq j \leqq 4$.

A possible generalization would be

$$(16) \qquad T_{F^k}(a_{jk}) = c_j + T_{F^k}(a_{j-1\ k-1}) - T_F(a_{j-1\ k-1}) \qquad 1 \leqq k \leqq j$$

This expression agrees with the others (and with a_{42} and a_{31} of *(15)*). Also, a_{jk} is uniquely defined by *(16)* since the right-hand side of *(16)* is positive (by *A2P1*).

Now, could it be that

$$(17) \qquad v_j(x) - x^+ = T_{F^k}(x^+) - T_{F^k}(a_{jk}) \qquad x \in D_{jk} \quad 1 \leqq k \leqq j$$

for any $j \geqq 1$, where a_{jk} and D_{jk} are defined as above (*(16)* and *(13)*)? Anyway, *(17)* is an example of a reasonable guess at what an explicit expression for $v_j(x)$ may look like.

That is the end of the report on how I found a sensible assumption on which to base a proof by induction. Fortunately the test of the hypothesis (using *(6)*) proved *(17)* to be a correct guess (see A5), so the process of finding a sensible assumption could stop here.

5.4.3 <u>The explicit solution</u>. A straight-forward statement of the solution can now be made (for a proof, see *A5P2* and *A5P2'*):

Explicit expressions for the sequence of functions $v_j(x)$, $j \geqq 1$, defined recursively by *(1')*, are given by

$$(18) \qquad v_j(x) = x^+ + T_{F^k}(x^+) - T_{F^k}(a_{jk}) \qquad x \in D_{jk} \quad 1 \leqq k \leqq j$$

where a_{jk} is defined by

$$(19) \qquad T_F^k(a_{jk}) = c_j + T_F^k(a_{j-1\ k-1}) - T_F(a_{j-1\ k-1}) \qquad 1 \leqq k \leqq j$$

$$(a_{j0} = 0 \text{ for } j \geqq 0 \text{ and } a_{jk} = 0 \text{ for } k > j)$$

and D_{jk} is the subset of the real line defined by

$$D_{j+1\ 1} = \bigcup_{k=1}^{j} [D_{jk} \cap \{x|x^+ > a_{jk}\}]$$

$$(20) \qquad D_{j+1\ k+1} = D_{jk} \cap \{x|x^+ \leqq a_{jk}\} \qquad 1 \leqq k \leqq j$$

$$D_{11} = R$$

See *(5.5.3 - 5)* for some of the properties of the a_{jk}:s that are immediate consequences of the definition *(19)* (cf *(16)*). As for the D_{jk}:s, note that $D_{jk} \cap \{x|x^+ \leqq a_{jk}\} = D_{jk} \cap \{x|v_j(x) - x^+ \geqq 0\}$ by *(18)* so that *(20)* is equivalent to *(13)*. Thus, for each $j \geqq 1$, the collection of sets D_{jk}, $1 \leqq k \leqq j$ form a partition of the set of real numbers (see under *(13)*).

To see that *(18)* is consistent with the corresponding expression in the constant-cost case, (3.5.2), suppose that $c_j = c$, $j \geqq 1$. Then $a_{j1} = v$, where v is defined by $T_F(v) = c$ (*A2D1*). Suppose $a_{jk} = v$ for some j, k such that $1 \leqq k \leqq j$. This is true for $k = 1$ and any $j \geqq 1$. Then, by *(19)*,

$$T_F^{k+1}(a_{j+1\ k+1}) = c + T_F^{k+1}(a_{jk}) - T_F(a_{jk})$$

where, by assumption, $c = T_F(a_{jk})$ which implies $a_{j+1\ k+1} = a_{jk}$ since T_F is strictly monotonic around a_{jk} (*A1P4*). Thus,

$$c_j \equiv c \Rightarrow a_{jk} \equiv v \qquad 1 \leqq k \leqq j$$

As for the sets D_{jk}, since $a_{jk} = v$, it follows from *(20)* (or from *(3)*, *(4)* and *(8)*) that

$$D_{11} = R \qquad D_{21} = \{x|x^+ > v\} \qquad D_{31} = \{x|x^+ > v\}$$

$$D_{22} = \{x|x^+ \leqq v\} \qquad D_{32} = \emptyset$$

$$D_{33} = \{x|x^+ \leqq v\}$$

Suppose there is some j for which $D_{j1} = D_{21}$, $D_{jj} = D_{22}$ and $D_{jk} = \emptyset$ for $2 \leqq k \leqq j-1$. Then, by *(20)*, $D_{j+1\ 1} = D_{21}$, $D_{j+1\ j+1} = D_{22}$, and $D_{j+1\ k+1} = \emptyset$ for $1 \leqq k \leqq j-1$. Since the assumption is true for $j = 2$, it then remains true for any $j > 2$. Thus, whatever j is, $v_j(x)$ will have no more than two branches, one for $x^+ \leqq v$ and one for $x^+ > v$.

In conclusion, if $c_j \equiv c$, $j \geqq 1$, then *(18)* can be written

$$(21) \qquad v_j(x) = \begin{cases} x^+ + T_{F^j}(x^+) - T_{F^j}(v) & x^+ \leqq v \\ x^+ + T_F(x^+) - T_F(v) & x^+ > v \end{cases} \qquad j \geqq 1$$

which is in complete agreement with *(3.5.2)*.

Now the two special cases, $c_j < c_{j-1} < \ldots < c_1$ and $c_j > c_{j-1} > \ldots > c_1$ will be examined.

5.5 RECALL - MONOTONIC UNIT COST

5.5.1 <u>Increasing unit cost</u>. The aim of this section is to find an explicit expression for $v_j(x)$ under the more restrictive assumption

$$(1) \qquad c_{j+1} < c_j \qquad j \geqq 1$$

that is, the cost per observation increases as you go on. A more conversational argument for the resulting decision rule will also be given.

By *(5.4.19)*, *(1)* is seen to be equivalent to

$$(2) \qquad a_{j1} < a_{j+1\ 1} \qquad j \geqq 1$$

since T_F is strictly decreasing to the left of a_{j1} (*A1P4*). Rewriting (*5.4.19*) as

$$(3) \qquad \int_{a_{jk}}^{a_{j+1\,1}} (1 - F(t))dt = \int_{a_{jk}}^{a_{j+1\,k+1}} (1 - F^{k+1}(t))dt \qquad 1 \leqq k \leqq j$$

the following implications are seen to hold

$$(4) \qquad a_{jk} < a_{j+1\,1} \Rightarrow a_{jk} < a_{j+1\,k+1} < a_{j+1\,1}$$

$$(5) \qquad a_{j+1\,1} < a_{jk} \Rightarrow a_{j+1\,1} < a_{j+1\,k+1} < a_{jk}$$

Then, since $a_{j1} < a_{j+1\,1}$ by (*2*), in this case it is always true (by (*4*)) that $a_{j1} < a_{j+1\,2} < a_{j+1\,1}$ and hence $a_{j+1\,2} < a_{j+2\,1}$ which ((*4*) again) implies $a_{j+1\,2} < a_{j+2\,3} < a_{j+2\,1}$. Now the first few a_{jk}:s can be ordered:

$$\begin{array}{ccccccccc}
a_{11} & & < & & a_{21} & & < & & a_{31} \\
\vdots & < & a_{22} & < & \vdots & < & a_{32} & < & \vdots \\
 & & \vdots & & < & a_{33} & < & & \vdots
\end{array}$$

Suppose that $a_{j-1\,k-1} < a_{jk} < a_{j1}$ for all values of k such that $1 < k \leqq j$ and for some value of $j > 1$. This is certainly true for $j = 2, 3$. Then $a_{jk} < a_{j+1\,1}$ so, by (*4*), $a_{jk} < a_{j+1\,k+1} < a_{j+1\,1}$. It follows by induction that

$$(6) \qquad a_{jk} < a_{j+1\,k+1} < a_{j+1\,1} \text{ for all } j,k \text{ such that } 1 \leqq k \leqq j$$

Making use of these results and the definition of D_{jk}, (*5.4.20*), it is seen that the first few D_{jk}:s are

$$\begin{array}{lll}
D_{11} = R & D_{21} = \{x \mid x^+ > a_{11}\} & D_{31} = \{x \mid x^+ > a_{21}\} \\
 & D_{22} = \{x \mid x^+ \leqq a_{11}\} & D_{32} = \{x \mid a_{11} < x^+ \leqq a_{21}\} \\
 & & D_{33} = \{x \mid x^+ \leqq a_{11}\}
\end{array}$$

Suppose that

$$D_{jj} = \{x|x^+ \leqq a_{11}\}$$

(7) $$D_{jk} = \{x|a_{j-k\ 1} < x^+ \leqq a_{j-k+1\ 1}\} \qquad 2 \leqq k \leqq j-1$$

$$D_{j1} = \{x|x^+ > a_{j-1\ 1}\}$$

for some value of $j > 1$. This is seen to be true for $j = 2, 3$. From *(6)* we have $a_{11} < a_{22} < \ldots < a_{jj}$ and $a_{j-k+1\ 1} < a_{j-k\ 2} < \ldots < a_{jk}$ for $1 \leqq k \leqq j$. Then *(7)* implies (using the definition of D_{jk}, *(5.4.20)*)
$D_{j+1\ j+1} = D_{jj} \cap \{x|x^+ \leqq a_{jj}\} = D_{jj}$ and
$D_{j+1\ k+1} = D_{jk} \cap \{x|x^+ \leqq a_{jk}\} = D_{jk}$ for $2 \leqq k \leqq j-1$ and
$D_{j+1\ 2} = D_{j1} \cap \{x|x^+ \leqq a_{j1}\} = \{x|a_{j-1\ 1} < x^+ \leqq a_{j1}\}$ and
$D_{j+1\ 1} = \bigcup_{k=1}^{j} [D_{jk} \cap \{x|x^+ > a_{jk}\}] = [D_{j1} \cap \{x|x^+ > a_{j1}\}] \cup \emptyset = \{x|x^+ > a_{j1}\}$.
from which it follows (by mathematical induction) that *(7)* holds true for $j > 1$.

Now the explicit expression for $v_j(x)$ in the general case, *(5.4.18)*, can be rewritten with *(7)* substituted for D_{jk}. Hence, if *(1)* holds, that is, if $c_{k+1} < c_k$, $k \geqq 1$, then $v_j(x)$ can be written in the following way:

(8) $$v_j(x) - x^+ = \begin{cases} T_{F^j}(x^+) - T_{F^j}(a_{jj}) & x^+ \leqq a_{11} \\ T_{F^{j-1}}(x^+) - T_{F^{j-1}}(a_{j\ j-1}) & a_{11} < x^+ < a_{21} \\ \vdots & \vdots \\ T_{F^k}(x^+) - T_{F^k}(a_{jk}) & a_{j-k\ 1} < x^+ \leqq a_{j-k+1\ 1} \\ \vdots & \vdots \\ T_{F^2}(x^+) - T_{F^2}(a_{j2}) & a_{j-2\ 1} < x^+ \leqq a_{j-1\ 1} \\ T_F(x^+) - T_F(a_{j1}) & a_{j-1\ 1} < x^+ \end{cases}$$

where $2 \leqq k \leqq j-1$.

If you are in (j,x), you should continue if $v_j(x) - x^+ \geqq 0$ and stop if

$v_j(x) - x^+ < 0$. Suppose $x \in D_{jk}$ for some value of k such that $2 \leqq k \leqq j$. Then, by (8) and (6), $x^+ \leqq a_{j-k+1\,1} < a_{jk} < a_{j1}$ and hence $v_j(x) - x^+ > 0$, so you should continue. On the other hand, supposing $x \in D_{j1}$, we find that $v_j(x) - x^+$ is non-negative if $a_{j-1\,1} < x^+ \leqq a_{j1}$ and negative if $x^+ > a_{j1}$. Thus, in a process with recall (and unchanged F) where $c_j < c_{j-1} < \ldots < c_1$, you should follow the decision rule

(9) If you are in (j,x), $j \geqq 1$, then <u>stop</u>, if $x^+ > a_{j1}$; <u>continue</u>, if $x^+ \leqq a_{j1}$

or one that is equivalent to it, that is, one that always tells you to do the same thing as (9) would have done. If $x^+ = a_{j1}$, then $v_j(x) - x^+ = 0$ so you should be indifferent to continuing or stopping. Here we adopt the convention that you continue in this case. This point is further discussed in connexion with (3.6.1).

Since $T_F(a_{j1}) = c_j$, it follows from (9) that you need only take the cost of the <u>next</u> observation into account when deciding whether to continue or to stop, if the cost of an observation increases as you proceed. By (3.6.1) this is true in the constant-cost case as well.

A more conversational argument that leads to the same conclusion can be modelled on the one that led to (3.6.1). Firstly, you should continue if your expected net gain from making just one more observation (as compared to stopping) is positive or zero (according to the convention stated above). Secondly, what you collect upon stopping is the greatest one of the values observed, since this is a process with recall.

If you are in (j,x), $j \geqq 1$, the next observation costs c_j. Your expected net gain from making just one more observation may then be written as $E\{\max(Y - x, 0)\} - c_j$. By A1P1(ii) and the definition of a_{j1}, this is equal to $T_F(x^+) - T_F(a_{j1})$ which is positive or zero <u>iff</u> $x^+ \leqq a_{j1}$. Thus, you should continue if $x^+ \leqq a_{j1}$. If $x^+ > a_{j1}$ you should stop, unless the <u>process</u> looks more favourable <u>after</u> the next observation. Since F is unchanged, this will be the case only if later observations (at least one of them) are less costly than the next one. However, by assumption the opposite is true: None of the future observations are less costly than the next one. Thus, you should stop if $x^+ > a_{j1}$, and once more *(9)* has been shown to be an optimal decision rule.

All you need to know to calculate a_{j1} is c_j and F. The unit costs of later observations should not influence your present decision, provided that they are increasing or constant. In fact, the above argument is seen to hold even under the weaker condition that they be none of them less than c_j. Thus, if you are in (j,x), $j \geqq 1$ and if no later observation is less costly than the next one, then the decision rule *(9)* is an optimal decision rule.

If you follow a myopic decision rule, you will use $x^+ + T_F(x^+) - c_j$ for your level of aspiration when in (j,x), $j \geqq 1$. You will then stop <u>iff</u> x^+ is greater than this quantity, which is seen to occur (see above) <u>iff</u> $x^+ < a_{j1}$. But this is exactly what *(9)* would have told you to do. Hence, a myopic decision rule is an optimal decision rule for a process with recall, if the cost per observation never decreases as you go on (that is, $c_j \leqq c_{j-1} \leqq \ldots \leqq c_1$, for each j).

5.5.2 <u>Decreasing unit cost</u>. The aim of this section is to find an explicit expression for $v_j(x)$ under the assumption

$$(10) \qquad c_{j+1} > c_j \qquad j \geqq 1$$

that is, the cost per observation decreases as you go on. A more conversational argument for the resulting decision rule will also be given.

By *(5.4.19)*, *(10)* is seen to be equivalent to (cf *(2)*).

$$(11) \qquad a_{j+1\,1} < a_{j1} \qquad j \geqq 1$$

Then, *(5)*, rewritten here as *(12)*, can be applied:

$$(12) \qquad a_{j+1\,1} < a_{jk} \Rightarrow a_{j+1\,1} < a_{j+1\,k+1} < a_{jk} \qquad 1 \leqq k \leqq j$$

By *(11)* $a_{j+1\,1} < a_{j1}$ so in this case $a_{j+1\,1} < a_{j+1\,2} < a_{j1}$ is seen to hold for $j \geqq 1$ by setting $k = 1$ in *(12)*. But *(11)* may be reformulated as $a_{j+2\,1} < a_{j+1\,1}$ so then we have $a_{j+2\,1} < a_{j+1\,2}$ and hence *(12)* may be applied again (set $k = 2$ and substitute $j+1$ for j) to give $a_{j+2\,1} < a_{j+2\,3} < a_{j+1\,2}$. Now the first few a_{jk}:s can be ordered:

$$\begin{array}{ccccccccc}
a_{31} & & < & & a_{21} & & < & & a_{11} \\
\vdots & < & a_{32} & < & \vdots & < & a_{22} & < & \vdots \\
\vdots & & < & & a_{33} & & < & & \vdots
\end{array}$$

Suppose that $a_{j1} < a_{jk} < a_{j-1\,k-1}$ for all values of k such that $1 < k \leqq j$ and for some value of $j > 1$. This is true for $j = 2, 3$. Then, by *(11)*, $a_{j+1\,1} < a_{jk}$ so that, by *(12)*, $a_{j+1\,1} < a_{j+1\,k+1} < a_{jk}$. We then have by induction (cf *(6)*),

$$(13) \qquad a_{j+1\,1} < a_{j+1\,k+1} < a_{jk} \text{ for all } j,k \text{ such that } 1 \leqq k \leqq j$$

Making use of *(6)* and the definition of D_{jk}, *(5.4.20)*, it is seen that the first few D_{jk}:s are (omitting $D_{11} = R$)

$$\begin{array}{lll}
D_{21} = \{x \mid x^+ > a_{11}\} & D_{31} = \{x \mid x^+ > a_{22}\} & D_{41} = \{x \mid x^+ > a_{33}\} \\
D_{22} = \{x \mid x^+ \leqq a_{11}\} & D_{32} = \emptyset & D_{42} = \emptyset \\
 & D_{33} = \{x \mid x^+ \leqq a_{22}\} & D_{43} = \emptyset \\
 & & D_{44} = \{x \mid x^+ \leqq a_{33}\}
\end{array}$$

Suppose that

$$(14) \qquad \begin{array}{ll}
D_{jj} = \{x \mid x^+ \leqq a_{j-1\,j-1}\} & \\
D_{jk} = \emptyset & 2 \leqq k \leqq j-1 \\
D_{j1} = \{x \mid x^+ > a_{j-1\,j-1}\} &
\end{array}$$

for some value of $j > 1$. This is seen to be true for $j = 2, 3$. By *(13)*, $a_{j1} < a_{jj} < a_{j-1\ j-1}$ for $j > 1$. Making use of this and *(5.4.20)*, *(14)* is seen to imply

$$D_{j+1\ j+1} = D_{jj} \cap \{x|x^+ \leqq a_{jj}\} = \{x|x^+ \leqq a_{jj}\}$$

$$D_{j+1\ k+1} = \emptyset \qquad 2 \leqq k \leqq j-1$$

$$D_{j+1\ 2} = D_{j1} \cap \{x|x^+ \leqq a_{j1}\} = \emptyset$$

$$D_{j+1\ 1} = \bigcup_{k=1}^{j} [D_{jk} \cap \{x|x^+ > a_{jk}\}] = [D_{j1} \cap \{x|x^+ > a_{j1}\}] \cup \emptyset \cup$$
$$\cup\ [D_{jj} \cap \{x|x^+ > a_{jj}\}] = \{x|x^+ > a_{jj}\}$$

Thus, *(14)* holds true for all $j > 1$.

Now the explicit expression for $v_j(x)$ in the general case, *(5.4.18)*, can be rewritten with *(14)* substituted for D_{jk}. Hence, if *(10)* holds, that is, if $c_{k+1} > c_k$, $k \geqq 1$, then $v_j(x)$ can be written in the following way:

$$\text{(15)} \qquad v_j(x) - x^+ = \begin{cases} T_{F^j}(x^+) - T_{F^j}(a_{jj}) & x^+ \leqq a_{j-1\ j-1} \\ T_F(x^+) - T_F(a_{j1}) & x^+ > a_{j-1\ j-1} \end{cases}$$

If you are in (j,x), $j \geqq 1$, you should continue if $v_j(x) - x^+ \geqq 0$ and stop if $v_j(x) - x^+ < 0$. If $x^+ \leqq a_{j-1\ j-1}$, the upper branch of *(15)* is valid, and then $v_j(x) - x^+$ is negative if $x^+ > a_{jj}$ and non-negative otherwise ($a_{jj} < a_{j-1\ j-1}$ by *(13)*). On the other hand, if $x^+ > a_{j-1\ j-1}$ then the lower branch holds and $v_j(x) - x^+$ is negative (since $a_{j-1\ j-1} > a_{j1}$ by *(13)*). This means that $v_j(x) - x^+$ is negative <u>iff</u> $x^+ > a_{jj}$. Thus, in a process with recall (and unchanged F) where $c_j > c_{j-1} > \ldots > c_1$, you should follow the decision rule

$$\text{(16)} \qquad \text{If you are in } (j,x),\ j \geqq 1, \text{ then } \begin{array}{ll} \underline{\text{stop}} \text{ if} & x^+ > a_{jj} \\ \underline{\text{continue}} \text{ if} & x^+ \leqq a_{jj} \end{array}$$

or one that is equivalent to it, that is, one that always tells you to do the same thing as *(16)* would have told you to do. As on previous occasions, we have adopted the convention that you continue in case of indifference to continuing or stopping. Cf *(9)* and the discussion in connexion with *(3.6.1)*.

If *(16)* is to be of any use, then the value of a_{jj} must be determined. By *(5.4.19)* this can be accomplished by using the relation

$$(17) \quad \begin{cases} T_{F^j}(a_{jj}) = c_j + T_{F^j}(a_{j-1\, j-1}) - T_F(a_{j-1\, j-1}) & j > 1 \\ T_F(a_{11}) = c_1 & \end{cases}$$

Thus, the <u>whole</u> sequence of numbers c_k, $1 \leqq k \leqq j$, must be taken into account when calculating a_{jj} (cf the comments to *(9)*). Moreover, the calculation will generally have to be done recursively since no explicit expression for the inverse of T_{F^j} is to be had, and hence none for a_{jj}, except in special cases. However, by *(13)* a_{jj} is bounded by the condition

$$(18) \quad a_{j1} < a_{jj} < a_{j-1\, j-1} < \dots < a_{11} \qquad j > 1$$

where a_{j1} is given by $T_F(a_{j1}) = c_j$. Thus, a_{jj} lies inside the interval bounded by a_{j1} and a_{11}, the length of which is seen to be directly related to $c_j - c_1$ (since $c_j - c_1 = T_F(a_{j1}) - T_F(a_{11})$ by definition). Cf the discussion at the end of Section 5.2.

We shall now give a more conversational argument in support of these results, the starting points of which are the same as in 5.5.1. Thus, you should continue if your expected net gain from making just one more observation is non-negative. If you are in (j,x), $j \geqq 1$, this occurs <u>iff</u> $x^+ \leqq a_{j1}$ (see 5.5.1). Moreover, since c_1 is the cost of the cheapest one of the future observations, you should stop if $x^+ > a_{11}$ by the argument of Section 5.2.

There now remains to be determined what you should do if you are in (j,x), $j > 1$ and $a_{j1} < x^+ \leqq a_{11}$. Making just one more observation is then an unfavourable thing to do, but, since $j > 1$ and later observations are cheaper than the next one, the expected loss from making the next observation, seen in isolation, may be expected to be recovered later on. Thus, if later observations are sufficiently less expensive than the next one, it may be advantageous to continue, even if continuing is an unfavourable thing to do on a one-period basis.

But what is to be meant by "sufficiently less"? Clearly, the unit cost of the whole sequence of possible future observations must be taken into account, and, depending on the values of all these costs (and on F) but on nothing else, there must be some number, z_j, $a_{j1} < z_j \leqq a_{11}$, acting as a break-even point, such that you should continue if $x^+ \leqq z_j$ and stop otherwise. If you are in $(1,x)$ the break-even point is a_{11}, so $z_1 = a_{11}$. Moreover, since costs are decreasing, the break-even point must be lower the further away you are from the "cheap" observations near the end of the process. Thus, $z_{k+1} < z_k$, $k \geqq 1$, so the z_j:s must satisfy the condition

$$a_{j1} < z_j < z_{j-1} < \ldots < z_1 = a_{11} \tag{19}$$

just like the a_{jj}:s do by *(18)*, and the decision rule that you should follow is

(20) If you are in (j,x), $j \geqq 1$, stop if $x^+ > z_j$; continue if $x^+ \leqq z_j$

This decision rule is seen to be the same as *(16)* if

$$z_j = a_{jj} \qquad j \geqq 1 \tag{21}$$

so what remains to be done is to show that *(21)* is at least plausible. It is true for $j = 1$, and by comparing *(19)* to *(18)* it is seen that it is not yet out of the question that it be true for $j > 1$ as well. However, *(17)* still needs to be justified. To see how this may be accomplished, we shall examine the simplest situation of this kind, that in which only two more observations can be made.

Suppose you are in $(2,x)$, $a_{21} < x^+ \leqq a_{11}$. If you had had only one observation at your disposal, you should have stopped there. Now you have two more, the last one of which is cheaper than the first ($c_2 > c_1$), so it may be advantageous to continue. For example, if the last observation is practically free ($c_1 \approx 0$), then the two of them together cost practically no more than the first one alone, so if you continue at all, you will probably want to make both of them; you will then have the possibility of choosing the best of two independent observations, $\max(Y_2, Y_1)$. To continue will then be the same as making one observation of this random variable, which has the distribution function F^2 (see A1.3). Your expected net gain from doing so (as compared to stopping) is then $T_{F^2}(x^+) - c_2$ which is greater than $T_F(x^+) - c_2$. Indeed, the process is looking more favourable when the whole future is taken into account (and not just the next observation).

The situation that you are facing in $(2,x)$ is illustrated by the following decision tree:

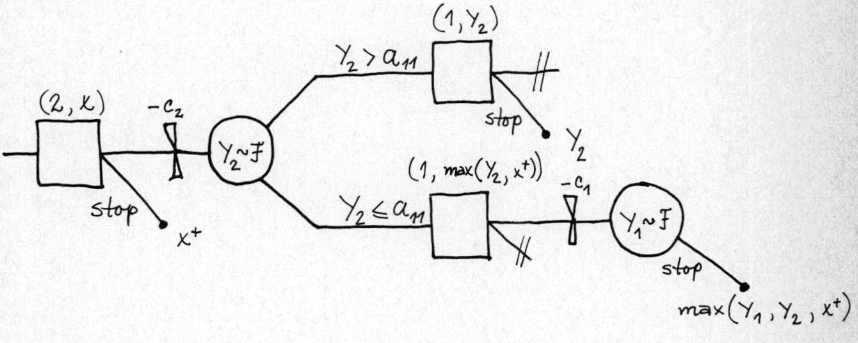

Figure 1 *Your situation when two periods remain*

You are in $(2,x)$, $a_{21} < x^+ \leqq a_{11}$. If you continue, you first pay c_2 and then observe Y_2, the value of which is determined by Chance according to the distribution function F. As a decision-maker you need only distinguish two events at this point: $Y_2 > a_{11}$ and $Y_2 \leqq a_{11}$. One of them must occur and both om them cannot.

If $Y_2 > a_{11}$ (the upper branch in the figure), you arrive in $(1,Y_2)$. You know that you should stop there (continue-branch barred) and collect Y_2. If $Y_2 \leqq a_{11}$ (lower branch), you arrive in state $(1,\max(Y_2,x^+))$ from which you know that you should continue (stop-branch barred) since $\max(Y_2,x^+) \leqq a_{11}$. You then pay c_1 and Chance gives you Y_1, again according to F and independently of Y_2. You are now in $(0,\max(Y_1, Y_2, x^+))$ so you are forced to stop and collect $\max(Y_1, Y_2, x^+)$.

Your expected net gain from continuing when in $(2,x)$, as before denoted by $v_2(x)$ can now be written as

$$(22) \qquad v_2(x) = - c_2 + P\{Y_2 > a_{11}\}E\{Y_2|Y_2 > a_{11}\} + \\ + P\{Y_2 \leqq a_{11}\}(- c_1 + E\{\max(Y_1, Y_2, x^+)|Y_2 \leqq a_{11}\})$$

Here it looks as if a conversational argument would have to end. The two probabilities in (22) are known: They are $1 - F(a_{11})$ and $F(a_{11})$, respectively; but what can be said about the two conditional expected values?

However, expressions for similar quantities have already been derived in 3.6 by a fairly conversational argument (starting after $(3.6.10)$). In fact, a look at that argument will show that exactly the wanted expressions are readily at hand. If a_{11} is substituted for v, and 2 for j, the argument that led to $(3.5.15)$ and $(3.6.16)$ is seen to imply

$$"P\{R_N > t|N = 1\}" = P\{Y_2 > t|Y_2 > a_{11}\}$$

and

$$"P\{R_N \leqq t|N = j = 2\}" = P\{\max(Y_1, Y_2, x^+) \leqq t|Y_2 \leqq a_{11}\}$$

where the quotation marks in the left hand sides indicate that the notation of Section 3.6 is being used.

Then $(3.6.17)$ and $(3.6.18)$ are directly applicable, and we get

$$(1 - F(a_{11}))E\{Y_2|Y_2 > a_{11}\} = a_{11}(1 - F(a_{11})) + T_F(a_{11})$$

and

$$F(a_{11})(-c_1 + E\{\max(Y_1, Y_2, x^+)|Y_2 \leqq a_{11}\}) =$$

$$= -c_1F(a_{11}) + a_{11}F(a_{11}) - \int_{x^+}^{a_{11}} F^2(t)dt + T_F(a_{11})F(a_{11}) =$$

$$= a_{11}F(a_{11}) + \int_{x^+}^{a_{11}} (1 - F^2(t))dt - (a_{11} - x^+) =$$

$$= x^+ + T_{F^2}(x^+) - T_{F^2}(a_{11}) - a_{11}(1 - F(a_{11})),$$

respectively, so *(22)* can be rewritten as

$$(23) \qquad v_2(x) - x^+ = T_{F^2}(x^+) - (c_2 + T_{F^2}(a_{11}) - T_F(a_{11}))$$

Since the condition $a_{21} < x^+$ has not been used, *(23)* holds for $x^+ \leqq a_{11}$. By definition z_2 must then satisfy the condition

$$(24) \qquad T_{F^2}(z_2) = c_2 + T_{F^2}(a_{11}) - T_F(a_{11})$$

so $z_2 = a_{22}$, by *(17)*. Moreover, *(23)* is seen to be identical to *(15)* for $j = 2$.

It has now been shown that $z_j = a_{jj}$ for $j = 1, 2$, and it should be clear how an argument (based on *(24)*) can be constructed that proves *(21)* by mathematical induction. This argument has already been provided (see *(5.4.16)* etc) so there is no need to repeat it. By now we consider *(16)* (as well as *(15)* and *(17)*) to be sufficiently justified.

In conclusion it may be noted that no myopic decision rule can be optimal in this case if $F(a_{jj}) \neq F(a_{j1})$ for some j (cf 5.3.3). Such a rule would tell you to continue <u>iff</u> $x^+ \leqq a_{j1}$ when you are in (j,x) whereas the "best" thing to do is to continue even if $a_{j1} < x^+ \leqq a_{jj}$. Thus, if your decision are only based on the prospects of the immediate future, you may be taking the wrong course of action since in this case the prospects of the whole process are always more favourable.

5.6 RECALL AND DISCOUNTING

In this section expressions will be given for $u_j(x)$, corresponding to those given in 5.4 and 5.5 for $v_j(x)$. A main result is the discovery of a new notation (generalizing T_F) by which the structural similarity between the cases with and without discounting is made apparent. The heuristics behind this result is described in detail. More conversational arguments for the plausibility of the explicit expressions for $u_j(x)$ can easily be modelled on those given previously (see 5.5 and 4.4.2) so they are omitted.

5.6.1 The general case. Starting from *(5.4.1)* which says

$$(1) \qquad \begin{cases} u_j(x) = -c_j + qE\{\max[\max(Y, x)^+, u_{j-1}(\max(Y, x))]\} \\ u_0(x) = x^+ \end{cases} \qquad j \geqq 1$$

an explicit expression for $u_j(x)$ can be derived by the same kind of argument as that of 5.4.2. The following notation will be used (cf *(5.4.19)* and *(5.4.20)*).

Definition b_{jk} is a solution of

$$(2) \qquad q^k T_{F^k}(b_{jk}) - (1 - q^k)b_{jk} = c_j + $$
$$+ q^k[T_{F^k}(b_{j-1\ k-1}) + b_{j-1\ k-1}] -$$
$$- q[T_F(b_{j-1\ k-1}) + b_{j-1\ k-1}] \qquad 1 \leqq k \leqq j$$

$$b_{j0} = 0 \text{ for } j \geqq 0 \text{ and } b_{jk} = 0 \text{ for } k > j$$

This defines b_{jk} uniquely; for a proof, see *A5P1*. If $q = 1$, *(2)* can be reduced to

$$T_{F^k}(b_{jk}) = c_j + T_{F^k}(b_{j-1\ k-1}) - T_F(b_{j-1\ k-1}) \qquad 1 \leqq k \leqq j$$

so in this case $b_{jk} = a_{jk}$ as it should be (see *(5.4.19)*).

Definition E_{jk} is the subset of the real line that satisfies

$$
\begin{aligned}
&E_{j+1\ 1} = \bigcup_{k=1}^{j} [E_{jk} \cap \{x | x^+ > b_{jk}\}] \\
(3)\qquad &E_{j+1\ k+1} = E_{jk} \cap \{x | x^+ \leqq b_{jk}\} \qquad 1 \leqq k \leqq j \\
&E_{11} = R
\end{aligned}
$$

For each $j \geqq 1$, the collection of sets E_{jk}, $1 \leqq k \leqq j$, form a partition of R; this is an immediate consequence of (3). If $q = 1$, it is seen from $(5.4.20)$ that $E_{jk} = D_{jk}$, since in this case $b_{jk} = a_{jk}$.

An explicit expression for $u_j(x)$ can now be written as

$$
(4)\qquad u_j(x) = x^+ + q^k[T_{F^k}(x^+) - T_{F^k}(b_{jk})] + (1 - q^k)(b_{jk} - x^+)
$$

$$
x \in E_{jk} \quad 1 \leqq k \leqq j
$$

See $A5P2$ for a proof; it is straight-forward using induction on j. If $q = 1$, (4) can be reduced to

$u_j(x) = x^+ + T_{F^k}(x^+) - T_{F^k}(b_{jk}) \qquad x \in E_{jk} \quad 1 \leqq k \leqq j$

where $b_{jk} = a_{jk}$ and $E_{jk} = D_{jk}$, so in this case $u_j(x) = v_j(x)$ as is to be expected (see $(5.4.18)$). Moreover, by $A3P3$ we have $- c_j \leqq u_j(x) \leqq v_j(x)$, $x \in R$, $j \geqq 1$, in agreement with the previous cases (cf 4.4.1 and $A4P10$, 4.3.2 and $A3P9$).

To see that (4) is consistent with the corresponding expression in the constant-cost case, $(4.4.5)$, suppose that $c_j = c$, $j \geqq 1$. Then $b_{j1} = u$ where u is defined by $qT_F(u) - (1 - q)u = c$, by (2) and $(4.4.6)$. Suppose $b_{j-1\ k-1} = u$ for some value of the subscripts such that (2) is applicable. This is true for $k = 2$ and any $j \geqq 2$. Then, by (2) and the definition of u,

$$
q^k T_{F^k}(b_{jk}) - (1 - q^k)b_{jk} = qT_F(u) - (1 - q)u + {}
$$

$$
+ q^k[T_{F^k}(u) + u] - q[T_F(u) + u]
$$

which can be rewritten as

$$q^k[T_{F^k}(b_{jk}) - T_{F^k}(u)] + (1 - q^k)(b_{jk} - u) = 0$$

from which it is seen that $b_{jk} = u$. By mathematical induction we then have

$$c_j \equiv c \Rightarrow b_{jk} = u \qquad 1 \leqq k \leqq j$$

As for the sets E_{jk}, since $b_{jk} = u$, the same argument as in 5.4.3 can be used, only with $b_{jk}(= u)$ substituted for $a_{jk}(= v)$. Hence, $E_{j1} = \{x|x^+ > u\}$, $E_{jj} = \{x|x^+ \leqq u\}$ and $E_{jk} = \emptyset$ for $2 \leqq k \leqq j-1$, by *(3)*.

In conclusion, if $c_j \equiv c$, $j \geqq 1$, then *(4)* can be written

$$(5) \qquad u_j(x) = \begin{cases} q^j[x^+ + T_{F^j}(x^+) - T_{F^j}(u)] + u(1 - q^j) & x^+ \leqq u \\ q[x^+ + T_F(x^+) - T_F(u)] + u(1 - q) & x^+ > u \end{cases}$$

which is in complete agreement with *(4.4.5)*.

5.6.2 Monotonic unit cost - a beginning. This subsection is a parallel to Section 5.5. The aim here is to derive explicit expressions for $u_j(x)$ under the assumption that c_j, $j \geqq 1$, be (strictly) monotonic. In 5.5 the major tools were the implications *(5.5.4)* and *(5.5.5)*, derived from a reformulation of *(5.4.19)*, the equation defining a_{jk}. This idea will now be carried over to the present case.

The defining equation of b_{jk}, *(2)*, may be written in the more symmetrical form (all subscripts increased by one step)

$$q \int_{b_{jk}}^{b_{j+1\,1}} (1 - F(t))dt + (1 - q)(b_{j-1\,1} - b_{jk}) =$$

$$= q^{k+1} \int_{b_{jk}}^{b_{j+1\,k+1}} (1 - F^{k+1}(t))dt + (1 - q^{k+1})(b_{j+1\,k+1} - b_{jk})$$

which can be reduced to

$$(6) \qquad \int_{b_{jk}}^{b_{j+1\,1}} (1 - qF(t))dt = \int_{b_{jk}}^{b_{j+1\,k+1}} (1 - q^{k+1}F^{k+1}(t))dt \quad \text{(cf (5.5.3))}$$

from which the desired implications are easily seen to hold:

(7) $b_{jk} < b_{j+1\ 1} \Rightarrow b_{jk} < b_{j+1\ k+1} < b_{j+1\ 1}$ (cf (5.5.4))

(8) $b_{j+1\ 1} < b_{jk} \Rightarrow b_{j+1\ 1} < b_{j+1\ k+1} < b_{jk}$ (cf (5.5.5))

Furthermore if $c_{j+1} < c_j$, $j \geqq 1$, it follows from *A2P8* that

(9) $b_{j1} < b_{j+1\ 1}$ $j \geqq 1$

since, by (3), $c_j = qT_F(b_{j1}) - (1 - q)b_{j1}$, $j \geqq 1$ (cf (5.3.4)). Similarly, $c_{j+1} > c_j$, $j \geqq 1$, is equivalent to

(10) $b_{j+1\ 1} < b_{j1}$ $j \geqq 1$

The form of these expressions is seen to be equal to that of their counterparts in 5.5; if "*a*" is called "*b*", then

(7) is equal to (5.5.4)
(8) " " " (5.5.5)
(9) " " " (5.5.2)
(10) " " " (5.5.11)

Moreover, the form of the definition of E_{jk} is equal to that of the definition of D_{jk}; if "*a*" is called "*b*", and "*D*" is called "*E*", then

(3) is equal to (5.4.20)

Then any consequence of the expressions on one side (above) is also a consequence of those on the other side; they do not differ in form, only in notation (and interpretation of course).

In particular, the sets E_{jk}, $1 \leqq k \leqq j$, will be equal to the corresponding sets D_{jk} of 5.5, if c_j, $j \geqq 1$ is monotonic, only with b_{jk} substituted for a_{jk}: By the above "dictionary", since (5.5.7) is a consequence of (5.5.2) $\wedge$ (5.5.4) $\wedge$ (5.4.20), then

$$E_{jj} = \{x | x^+ \leqq b_{11}\}$$

(11) $$E_{jk} = \{x | b_{j-k\ 1} < x^+ \leqq b_{j-k+1\ 1}\} \qquad 2 \leqq k \leqq j-1$$

$$E_{j1} = \{x | x^+ > b_{j-1\ 1}\}$$

which only differs in notation from *(5.5.7)*, must be a consequence of *(9)* ∧ *(7)* ∧ *(3)*. Similarly, since *(5.5.14)* is a consequence of *(5.5.11)* ∧ *(5.5.5)* ∧ *(5.4.20)*, then

$$E_{jj} = \{x | x^+ \leqq b_{j-1\ j-1}\}$$

(12) $$E_{jk} = \emptyset \qquad 2 \leqq k \leqq j-1$$

$$E_{j1} = \{x | x^+ > b_{j-1\ j-1}\}$$

follows from *(10)* ∧ *(8)* ∧ *(3)*.

An explicit expression for $u_j(x)$ can now be given by use of *(4)* ∧ *(11)* and *(4)* ∧ *(12)* for the two cases $c_{j+1} < c_j$ and $c_{j+1} > c_j$, $j \geqq 1$, respectively. It will be clear by now what these expressions will look like; they are, as *(4)* is, rather messy. So, before stating them, it may be worthwhile to see whether *(4)* can be brought on the same form as *(5.4.18)*. In order to achieve this, it may be enough to bring (2) on the same form as *(5.4.19)* since *(3)* is already equal in form to *(5.4.20)*.

Let us return to the general case and see whether the structural similarities between the various expressions in the two cases <u>with</u> and <u>without</u> discounting can be further exploited.

5.6.3 <u>The general case again - new notation</u>. It was seen before that *(5.4.19)* could be written as

(13) $$T_F(a_{jk}) - T_F(a_{j+1\ 1}) = T_{F^{k+1}}(a_{jk}) - T_{F^{k+1}}(a_{j+1\ k+1})$$

This is just *(5.5.3)* again. To see the similarity of *(13)* to its counterpart in the discounting case, *(6)*, let us introduce the notation

$$(14) \qquad \int_s^{s'} (1 - qF(t))dt = T_F^q(s) - T_F^q(s') \qquad s, s' \text{ real numbers}$$

or, more generally,

$$(14') \qquad \int_s^{s'} (1 - q^k F^k(t)dt = T^q_{F^k}(s) - T^q_{F^k}(s') \qquad k \geq 1$$

which is seen to agree with *A1D1*, the definition of T_F, for $q = 1$, in which case the q:s can be dropped. (Note that "q" in $T^q_{F^k}$ is just a superscript. It must not be interpreted as an exponent. This notation has been chosen for typographical reasons. A symbol such as $T_{(qF)^k}$ may be preferable from other points of view but it yields too clumsy expressions in my opinion.) Then *(6)* can be rewritten as

$$(15) \qquad T_F^q(b_{jk}) - T_F^q(b_{j+1\ 1}) = T^q_{F^{k+1}}(b_{jk}) - T^q_{F^{k+1}}(b_{j+1\ k+1})$$

which is seen to have the same form as *(13)*; if "a" is called "b" and "T_F" is called "T_F^q" (or "F" is called "qF"), then *(13)* is equal to *(15)* and hence

(2) is equal to *(5.4.19)*

The next thing to be done is to apply *(14)* to *(4)* and see whether the same kind of similarity holds between *(4)* and *(5.4.18)*. *(4)* can be rewritten as

$$u_j(x) = x^+ + q^k \int_{x^+}^{b_{jk}} (1 - F^k(t))dt + (1 - q^k)(b_{jk} - x^+) =$$

$$= x^+ + \int_{x^+}^{b_{jk}} (1 - q^k F^k(t))dt \qquad x \in E_{jk}$$

which yields, by *(14)*

$$(16) \qquad u_j(x) = x^+ + T^q_{F^k}(x^+) - T^q_{F^k}(b_{jk}) \qquad x \in E_{jk} \quad 1 \leq k \leq j$$

(16) is seen to have the same form as *(5.4.18)*; if "a" is called "b" and "F" is called "qF", they are equal, and hence

(4) is equal to *(5.4.18)*

Let us now attempt to define T_F^q in such a way that *(14)* holds. Clearly any "good" definition of T_F^q should be consistent with the definitions of b_{j1} and a_{j1} (or those of u and v; see *A2D2* and *A2D1* or the context of Figure 3 of Section 4.3). We have, by *(2)*,

$$(17) \qquad qT_F(b_{j1}) = c_j + (1-q)b_{j1} \qquad j \geqq 1$$

whereas, by *(5.4.19)*

$$(18) \qquad T_F(a_{j1}) = c_j \qquad j \geqq 1$$

Then $T_F^q(s)$ should be defined in such a way that

$$(19) \qquad T_F^q(b_{j1}) = c_j \qquad j \geqq 1$$

holds true, whatever value b_{j1} (or the positive numbers c_j) may assume. Thus by *(19)* and *(17)*, define $T_F^q(s)$ by

$$(20) \qquad T_F^q(s) = qT_F(s) - (1-q)s \qquad 0 < q \leqq 1, \quad s \in R$$

where F is a distribution function such that $T_F(s)$ is defined by *A1D1*. We then have

$$T_F^q(s) - T_F^q(s') = q\int_s^{s'} (1 - F(t))dt + (1 - q)(s' - s) =$$

$$= s' - s - \int_s^{s'} qF(t)dt = \int_s^{s'} (1 - qF(t))dt,$$

that is, *(14)*. In all, *(20)* seems to behave as a "good" definition of T_F^q should. Note that T_F^q is the same function as H, defined in the proof of *A2P8*. Hence the properties of T_F^q may be derived from the contents of **A2** and **A1**.

More generally, let us define $T^q_{F^k}$ by

$$(21) \qquad T^q_{F^k}(s) = q^k T_{F^k}(s) - (1 - q^k)s \qquad 0 < q \leqq 1, \quad s \in R, \quad k \geqq 1$$

which is easily seen to be consistent with *(20)* and *(14')*.

Thus, the explicit expression for $u_j(x)$ given by *(16)* makes sense. This means that the following short-cut is justified: Any expression that can be derived directly from the explicit expression for $v_j(x)$ can be generalized to hold for $u_j(x)$ by simply substituting "b" for "a", "E" for "D", and "qF" for "F" (and "u" for "v", of course!). More formally (and extended a bit): Let A be any correct expression in the no-discounting case, and let $B = f(A)$ be the (unique) expression that is obtained from A by making the above substitutions. Then B is a correct expression in the discounting case. Moreover, if $A \Rightarrow A'$, then $B \Rightarrow B'$, where $B' = f(A')$. (Clearly, starting with B, $f^{-1}(B) = A$ uniquely etc. so the two cases are <u>isomorphic</u>.)

By *A1P1* it is clear that $T_F(s)$ might as well have been defined by

$$(22) \qquad s + T_F(s) = E\{\max(Y, s)\}$$

where F is the distribution function of Y. Then, by *(20)*, $T_F^q(s)$ can as well be defined by

$$(23) \qquad s + T_F^q(s) = qE\{\max(Y, s)\}$$

Since *(23)* is equal to *(22)* for $q=1$, it is apparent how T_F^q can be defined as an extension of T_F. In fact this is exactly what is being done by *(23)*. (A definition similar to *A1D1* can also be given.)

How $T_F^q(s)$ can be interpreted is another thing that is made apparent by *(23)*. Suppose you are in (j,x), $j \geqq 1$. Then $x^+ + T_F^q(x^+)$ denotes the expected present value of what you will collect if you make just one more observation. Since you will receive x^+ if you stop where you are, $T_F^q(x^+)$ denotes the improvement of the expected present value of what you will collect, if you make just one more observation rather than to stop. The corresponding interpretations of $T_F(s)$ are seen to be obtained by writing "value" instead of "present value" in the preceding sentences.

Things are beginning to fit nicely together. The kind of equivalence that holds between the model for the case without discounting and that for the case with it has been discovered. Now it is easy to state an explicit expression for $u_j(x)$ (in the general case as well as in the two cases of monotonic unit cost) from a knowledge of one for $v_j(x)$.

5.6.4 The explicit expressions. The results of the preceding subsections will now be applied, first to the expressions in 5.4.3 which cover the general case, and then to the expressions in 5.5 which cover the two cases of monotonic unit cost.

In the general case, (5.4.18), (5.4.19) and (5.4.20) are transformed into the following expressions for the case with discounting:

$$(24) \qquad u_j(x) = x^+ + T_F^q(x^+) - T_F^q(b_{jk}) \qquad x \in E_{jk}, \quad 1 \leqq k \leqq j$$

where b_{jk} is defined by

$$(25) \qquad T_F^q(b_{jk}) = c_j + T_F^{q}{}^{k}(b_{j-1\ k-1}) - T_F(b_{j-1\ k-1}) \qquad 1 \leqq k \leqq j$$

$$(b_{j0} = 0 \text{ for } j \geqq 0 \text{ and } b_{jk} = 0 \text{ for } k > j)$$

and E_{jk} is the subset of the real line defined by

$$E_{j+1\ 1} = \bigcup_{k=1}^{j} [E_{jk} \cap \{x | x^+ > b_{jk}\}]$$

$$(26) \qquad E_{j+1\ k+1} = E_{jk} \cap \{x | x^+ \leqq b_{jk}\} \qquad 1 \leqq k \leqq j$$

$$E_{11} = R$$

By (14) or (20) they are equal to (4), (2) and (3), respectively.

In the case of increasing unit cost, $c_{j+1} < c_j$, $j \geqq 1$, (5.5.8) is transformed into (see also (5.6.11))

$$
(27)\qquad u_j(x) - x^+ = \begin{cases} T^q_{F^j}(x^+) - T^q_{F^j}(b_{jj}) & x^+ \leqq b_{11} \\ T^q_{F^{j-1}}(x^+) - T^q_{F^{j-1}}(b_{j\ j-1}) & b_{11} < x^+ \leqq b_{21} \\ \vdots & \vdots \\ T^q_{F^k}(x^+) - T_{F^k}(b_{jk}) & b_{j-k\ 1} < x^+ \leqq b_{j-k+1\ 1} \\ \vdots & \vdots \\ T^q_{F^2}(x^+) - T^q_{F^2}(b_{j2}) & b_{j-2\ 1} < x^+ \leqq b_{j-1\ 1} \\ T^q_F(x^+) - T^q_F(b_{j1}) & b_{j-1\ 1} < x^+ \end{cases}
$$

where $2 \leqq k \leqq j-1$. You should then follow the decision rule

$$
(28)\qquad \text{If you are in } (j,x),\ j \geqq 1, \text{ then } \begin{array}{ll} \underline{\text{stop}} \text{ if} & x^+ > b_{j1} \\ \underline{\text{continue}} \text{ if} & x^+ \leqq b_{j1} \end{array}
$$

which can be obtained by transforming *(5.5.9)* or as a consequence of *(27)*. It will be seen that *(28)* is a myopic decision rule.

In the case of decreasing unit cost, $c_{j+1} > c_j$, $j \geqq 1$, *(5.5.15)* is transformed into (see also *(5.6.12)*)

$$
(29)\qquad u_j(x) - x^+ = \begin{cases} T^q_{F^j}(x^+) - T^q_{F^j}(b_{jj}) & x^+ \leqq b_{j-1\ j-1} \\ T^q_F(x^+) - T^q_F(b_{j1}) & x^+ > b_{j-1\ j-1} \end{cases}
$$

and you should follow the decision rule

$$
(30)\qquad \text{If you are in } (j,x),\ j \geqq 1, \text{ then } \begin{array}{ll} \underline{\text{stop}} \text{ if} & x^+ > b_{jj} \\ \underline{\text{continue}} \text{ if} & x^+ \leqq b_{jj} \end{array}
$$

which can be obtained by transforming *(5.5.16)* or as a consequence of *(29)*. It will be seen that *(29)* is not a myopic decision rule unless $F(b_{jj}) = F(b_{j1})$ for all relevant values of j (cf the last paragraph of 5.5.2).

5.6.5 A concluding comment. The main result of this section is not the derivation of various explicit expressions for $u_j(x)$ but rather the discovery of the exact form of the structural similarity between (the expressions of) the two cases with and without discounting. Given an expression that holds true in the no-discounting case, it is usually difficult (not to say impossible) to "see" just from the look of it exactly how it will be transformed if discounting is taken into consideration (this is no problem the other way around). However, when it comes to the models treated in this book, it is now a simple matter to perform the correct transformation, for this amounts to taking the expression for the no-discounting case and substituting

T^q for T
u " v
b " a
E " D

(It is enough to substitute T^q for T if we keep in mind that discounting is being taken into account. Since we have used separate notation in the two cases, here the other substitutions must be performed as well.)

We have found this to work for a process with recall and it is easily seen that it works for a process without recall as well. For example, set $q = 1$ in *(5.3.1)* to get its no-discounting counterpart:

$$(31) \qquad v_j = - c_j + E\{\max(Y, v^+_{j-1})\}$$

which may be rewritten as

$$(32) \qquad v_j = v^+_{j-1} + T_F(v^+_{j-1}) - c_j$$

If u is substituted for v and T^q for T in *(32)*, we get

$$(33) \qquad u_j = u^+_{j-1} + T^q_F(u^+_{j-1}) - c_j$$

which, by *(22)*, is the same as

$$(34) \qquad u_j = - c_j + qE\{\max(Y, u^+_{j-1})\}$$

which is (5.3.1) again. It works.

5.7 CONCLUSION

We have now studied the consequences of letting the cost of an observation be variable rather than constant. In state (j,x), $j \geqq 1$, you are then facing a sequence of costs, c_k, $1 \leqq k \leqq j$, all of which may be different, where c_j denotes the cost of the next observation and so on.

In a process without recall (and without discounting) you should still follow a decision rule of the form (cf (2.5.1))

$$(1) \qquad \text{If you are in } (j,x),\ j \geqq 1, \text{ then } \begin{array}{ll} \text{stop} & \text{if } x^+ > v_j \\ \text{continue} & \text{if } x^+ < v_j \end{array}$$

where v_j may be determined (recursively) by use of (5.3.2) (set $q = 1$; note that v_j of (1) is not the same as that of (2.5.1) although they may be given similar interpretations; see 5.2). If the cost per observation increases as you continue, the optimal levels of aspiration have the same properties of monotonicity as in the constant-cost case. If the cost per observations decreases, this is no longer true. The levels of aspiration may then increase as you approach the point of forced stopping (see (5.3.24)). In either case no myopic decision rule is optimal unless $F(v_j-) = F(v'_j)$ (v'_j denotes the myopic level of aspiration) for all relevant values of j (cf 3.8).

In a process with recall (but still without discounting) you should follow a decision rule of the form

$$(2) \qquad \text{If you are in } (j,x),\ j \geqq 1, \text{ then } \begin{array}{ll} \text{stop} & \text{if } x^+ > v_j(x) \\ \text{continue} & \text{if } x^+ < v_j(x) \end{array}$$

where $v_j(x)$ may be calculated by use of (5.4.18). (As above, this is not the same $v_j(x)$ as in (3.9.1); see 5.2.) However, the expression for $v_j(x)$ has j branches, one for each of the sets D_{jk}, $1 \leqq k \leqq j$ (which form a partition of the set of real numbers; see (5.4.20)). If $x \in D_{jk}$, then $v_j(x) - x^+$ has the same sign as $a_{jk} - x^+$, where a_{jk} may be determined recursively by use of (5.4.19) given F and the set of future costs. Thus, rule (2) is equivalent to

$$(3) \qquad \text{If you are in } (j,x),\ j \geqq 1,\ x \in D_{jk}, \quad \begin{cases} \underline{\text{stop}} & \text{if } x^+ > a_{jk} \\ \underline{\text{continue}} & \text{if } x^+ < a_{jk} \end{cases}$$

In this sense a_{jk} is a counterpart of v of the constant-cost case (cf (3.8.1) and (3.8.2)). The following interpretation of D_{jk} is strongly suggested by the material in 5.4 and 5.5: If you are in (j,x), $j \geqq 1$, $x \in D_{jk}$, you should stop after having made at the most k further observations, even though you may not be forced to stop there ($1 \leqq k \leqq j$). The sequence of future costs is then such that you should not continue beyond $(k,\cdot)$ if you have already made an observation the value of which is x.

If the cost per observation increases as you continue, $v_j(x)$ still has j branches, but their domains, the sets D_{jk}, assume a particularly simple form (see (5.5.8)). An optimal decision rule is then obtained by using a_{j1} for level of aspiration when in (j,x). However, a_{j1} is also the myopic level of aspiration, so a myopic decision rule is also optimal. Moreover, a_{j1} is related to F and c_j in exactly the same way as v is to F and c. The situation is then similar to that of the constant-cost case. Thus, a myopic decision rule is optimal for a process with recall if future costs are non-decreasing (see 5.5.1).

If the cost per observation decreases as you continue, $v_j(x)$ can be calculated from (5.5.15). It has then only two branches (as in the constant-cost case), one for D_{j1} and one for D_{jj}, all other D_{jk}:s being empty. Whatever state you are in, if the next observation seems worth making, there is nothing to indicate *a priori* that you should stop before having made all the remaining ones (cf the above interpretation of D_{jk}); otherwise you should stop at once. This is also reflected in the alternative optimal decision rule (5.5.16) which uses a_{jj} for level of aspiration. Since a_{jj} must be determined recursively starting from a_{11}, a_{22} and so on, this decision rule takes account of the whole future and not just the cost of the next observation. This is as it should be, since here the cost per observation decreases as you go on, so the prospects of the whole future may be good even if those of the near future are bad. As a consequence, $a_{jj} > a_{j1}$, $j > 1$, so no myopic decision rule is optimal unless $F(a_{jj}-) = F(a_{j1})$ for all relevant values of j (see 5.5.2).

Similar results hold if discounting is taken into consideration. Moreover, in 5.6 we discovered a procedure by which it is possible to generalize any expression for the no-discounting case to the corresponding expression for the discounting case (see 5.6.5). Essentially, the introduction of discounting amounts to a contraction of the optimal levels of aspiration, just as we found in Chapter 4 for the constant-cost case.

Let us now examine the property of a constant-cost process which made us relax the assumption of the cost of an observation being always the same. It says (see 3.9)

- You should participate (buy at least one ticket) in a lottery of this kind if and only if it is favourable to participate on a one-period basis, i.e. on the condition that you may only buy one ticket.

As was to be expected this is false if the cost per observation decreases as you go on.

6 Conclusion

In line with the purpose of this work, the chosen set of optimal stopping problems has been subject to a detailed study, including alternative derivations of the central results or arguments for their plausibility. Starting with the basic models, the experience and insight gained by studying them were subsequently used for deriving corresponding results in the more general situation in which costs vary over time. Optimal decision rules were derived and some of their properties were examined for the two special cases of increasing and decreasing cost per observation. A procedure was found for transforming any expression for the no-discounting cases into its counterpart for the discounting cases. These results and their interpretation (Chapter 5) constitute the main achievement of this study.

In all cases, an optimal decision rule can be reformulated so as to be equivalent to a rule which tells you to stop when you have observed a "satisfactory" result, one in excess of a given level of aspiration, as determined by the decision rule. You should behave as if you were "satisficing". This is an optimal way of behaving since the cost of continuing is taken into account when determining the level of aspiration. Cf March & Simon (1958, pp 140-1). The value of the level of aspiration may or may not vary according to the state in which you are, depending upon the particular case (cf *ibid* pp 48-50). The introduction of discounting essentially amounts to a contraction of the optimal levels of aspiration; their properties of monotonicity remain the same as in the corresponding cases without discounting.

In the cases with recall, a myopic decision rule is optimal if the cost per observation never decreases as you continue. However, if the cost per observation decreases as you go on, you may arrive in a state where a myopic decision rule will tell you to stop whereas the best thing to do is to continue. The same is true in the cases with no recall, whether costs decrease, increase or remain equal (see 5.7). It would be interesting to attempt to extend these results towards an eventual characterization of the set of stopping problems for which myopic behaviour is optimal. In economic terms, these situations are such that the more favourable action will always be chosen even if decisions are only based on the prospects of the immediate future. See DeGroot(1970), Sections 13.10 and 13.18, for results in this direction.

The following variations of the problems discussed can all be treated within the framework of analysis that has been used in this work. Suppose you may make more than one observation in each period, always with recall within the period. If you can only make exactly k observations at one time, then all previous results are directly applicable by simply substituting F^k for F everywhere (see A1.3). If k varies form period to period, the results are not so easily transferred since the distribution function is then no longer stationary (see 1.5). However, the recursive relations may easily be adapted to this assumption if you know the appropriate distribution function for each future period. If they differ, the situation is similar to the one with variable cost per observation and may be regarded as a sequence of different one-period processes.

An interesting problem with a comparable structure has been treated by MacQueen(1964): You obtain only preliminary information about the value of an observation at the time of making it. You may then stop and take it, continue and leave it (no recall) or, at a cost, perform a test and obtain more information about its value. If you decide to test, then after having obtained the additional information, you may again either stop or continue. No more than one test may be performed in each period. The situation is interpreted in the terms of buying a house (see ii. in 1.1). This is like having two processes "intertwined", a main one regarding stopping and continuing, and a secondary one regarding testing. A more general problem with this structure has been treated by Marschak and Yahav(1966) with the management of a development project in mind (see iii. in 1.1). The article by Hess(1962) is also relevant in this context.

The constant interplay between mathematical and economic arguments is at the core of this study. Most of the results have been obtained by this cross-breeding of ideas, concepts and ways of drawing conclusions from two fields. In the words of the introduction (see 1.4), "mathematical intuition" has been used to amplify "economic intuition", and *vice versa*. Problems of an economic content have been transformed into mathematical problems; the structure of the mathematical solution gave rise to some further <u>mathematical</u> questions being asked and treated; in turn the results, when translated back into the terms of the original (economic) problem, could be made richer in content than was to be expected at the outset. Moreover, the effort of justifying these results by more direct arguments may be said to have led to a deeper understanding of the situations discussed. Thus, a better starting point is available (in the form of principal arguements, notation etc.) for the understanding of situations of the same general structure from an economic point of view.

A1 The Transform T_F

A1.1 INTRODUCTION

Let X be a random variable with distribution function F and finite mean (this condition will be weakened in the next section). Define the real-valued function T_F on the real line by

$$(1) \qquad T_F(s) = \int_s^\infty (1 - F(t))dt \qquad s \in R$$

Geometrically, $T_F(s)$ stands for the area between $y = 1$ and the curve $y = F(t)$ and to the right of $t = s$ (see Figure 1).

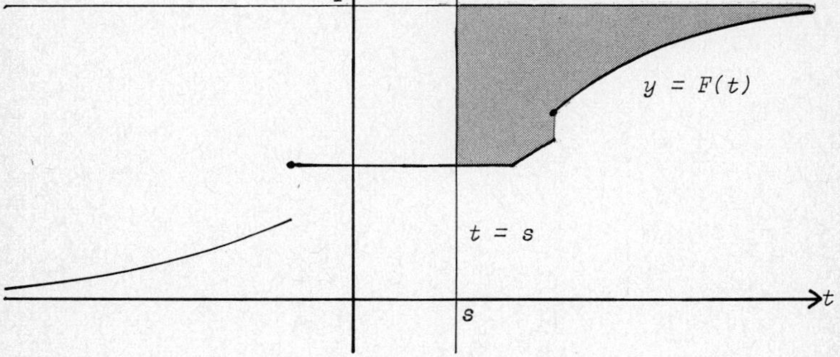

Figure 1 *A geometrical representation of* $T_F(s)$

Recall that the mean of X may be defined by

$$(2)\qquad E\{X\} = \int_0^\infty (1 - F(t))dt - \int_{-\infty}^{0} F(t)dt$$

where the mean is said to be finite or to exist if and only if both integrals exist (see e g Tucker [1962 p 81]). This definition is equivalent to the ones more commonly encountered that make use of the density function or the frequency function of the random variable in question. By using the distribution function, however, there is no need to make a notational distinction between "continuous" and "discrete" random variables nor is there any need for even more cumbersome expressions in the case when the random variable is of a more general kind. Also, the geometrical interpretation of $E\{X\}$ as defined by *(2)* is immediately clear in analogy to *(1)* and Figure 1.

The reason for introducing $T_F(s)$ is to have a concise notation for expressions like $E\{\max(X,s)\}$, where s is a real number and X is an arbitrary random variable having a finite mean. Note that

$$(3)\qquad \max(X,s) = \begin{cases} X & \text{if } X > s \\ s & \text{if } X \leqq s \end{cases}$$

so that $P\{\max(X,s) \leqq t\} = P\{X \leqq t \wedge s \leqq t\}$ which is equal to $P\{X \leqq t\}$ if $s \leqq t$ and zero otherwise. Thus the value of the distribution function of $\max(X,s)$, say $F_s(t)$, is identically zero for $t < s$ and equal to $F(t)$ otherwise, that is

$$(4)\qquad F_s(t) = P\{\max(X,s) \leqq t\} = \begin{cases} 0 & t < s \\ F(t) & t \geqq s \end{cases}$$

By *(2)* and *(4)* $E\{\max(X,s)\}$ may be derived geometrically from Figure 2:

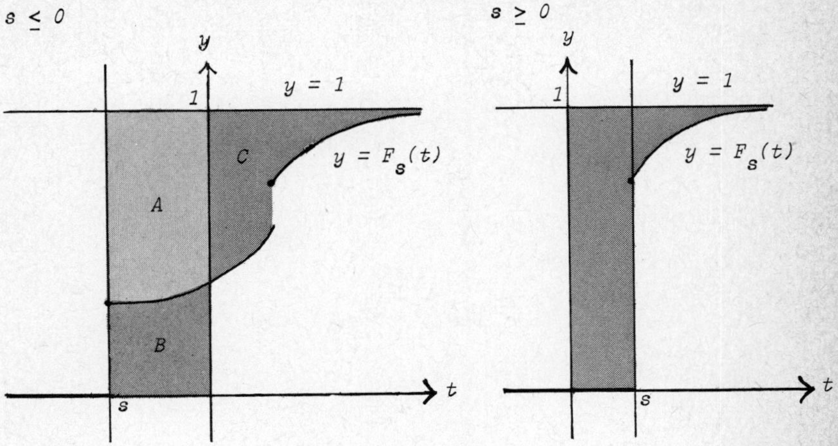

Figure 2 *A geometrical representation of* $E\{\max(X,s)\}$

From the left hand side of Figure 2, the case $s \leqq 0$, it follows that $E\{\max(X,s)\}$ is equal to $C - B$. But $C - B$ may be written as $(A + C) - (A + B)$. Now, $A + C$ is equal to $T_F(s)$ from *(1)* and Figure 1 and $A + B$ is equal to $-s$(from Figure 2; recall that s is negative) so for $s \leqq 0$

$$(5) \qquad E\{\max(X,s)\} = s + T_F(s)$$

From the right hand side of Figure 2, the case $s > 0$, it follows immediately that *(5)* holds. Thus, the definition *(1)* implies *(5)*.

From *(5)* it is clear that $T_F(s) = E\{\max(X,s)\} - s$. But from *(3)* it follows that $\max(X,s) - s = \max(X - s, 0)$. Hence *(5)* implies

$$(6) \qquad T_F(s) = E\{\max(X - s,\ 0)\}$$

Let *(6)* be given and set Y equal to $\max(X - s,\ 0)$. Then $Y \geqq 0$ so that the distribution function of Y is identically zero for all negative arguments and by *(2)*

$$(7) \qquad E\{Y\} = \int_0^\infty (1 - P\{Y \leqq t\})dt = \int_0^\infty P\{Y > t\}dt$$

But $P\{Y > t\} = P\{X - s > t \vee 0 > t\} = P\{X > s + t \vee t < 0\}$ so that

$$P\{Y > t\} = \begin{cases} 1 & t < 0 \\ 1 - F(s+t) & t \geqq 0 \end{cases}$$ which by *(6)* and *(7)* gives

$$(8) \qquad T_F(s) = E\{Y\} = \int_0^\infty (1 - F(s+t))dt = \int_s^\infty (1 - F(t))dt$$

Hence, *(6)* implies *(1)* and the following closed circuit of implications has been shown to hold

$$\begin{array}{ccc} (1) & \Rightarrow & (5) \\ \nwarrow & & \swarrow \\ & (6) & \end{array}$$

Thus, any one of the expressions *(1)*, *(5)* and *(6)* implies the other two and the circuit of implications works the other way around as well:

$$\begin{array}{ccc} (1) & \Leftrightarrow & (5) \\ \searrow & & \nearrow \\ & (6) & \end{array}$$

Since they are equivalent, any one of the expressions may serve as a definition of $T_F(s)$: sometimes one of them is easier to handle than the others; however, the choice does not influence later results.

A1.2 ASSUMPTIONS AND PROPOSITIONS

Let X be a random variable with distribution function F and such that $E\{\max(X,0)\}$ is finite. Then there exists a function T_F defined by

$$\text{A1D1} \qquad T_F(s) = \int_s^\infty (1 - F(t))dt \qquad s \in R$$

where R stands for the set of real numbers. Thus T_F may be regarded as a transform of the distribution function F. Moreover, it is clear from the previous section that

A1P1 The following expressions are equivalent:

(i) $T_F(s) = \int_s^\infty (1 - F(t))dt$

(ii) $T_F(s) = E\{\max(X - s, 0)\}$

(iii) $E\{\max(X,s)\} = s + T_F(s)$

$T_F(s)$ has the following properties

A1P2 $T_F(s)$ *is non-negative*

A1P3 $T_F(s)$ *is non-increasing*

These propositions can be made more precise. Let $b = \inf\{s \mid F(s) = 1\}$ so that b stands for the smallest number such that $F(s) = 1$ for any $s > b$ (b may be infinite). Then

A1P4 $T_F(s)$ *is positive and strictly decreasing for* $s < b$ *and identically zero for* $s \geq b$

A1P5 $T_F(s)$ *is continuous*

A1P6 $T_F(s)$ *is convex*

Thus the curve $y = T_F(s)$ consists of an unbroken chain of line-segments and/or U-shaped arcs. The curve slopes downward and approaches the horizontal axis from above. Just how it slopes is made precise by the following two propositions:

A1P7 $T_F(s)$ *is differentiable for all* s *for which* $F(s)$ *is continuous*

A1P8 $T_F(s)$ *has a right hand derivative everywhere, the value of which is* $-(1 - F(s))$ *at the point* s

Clearly $T_F(s)$ has a left hand derivative as well, the value of which differs from that of the right hand derivative only for those values of s for which $F(s)$ is discontinuous. However, since by convention distribution functions are right hand continuous, notation is made simpler by using the right hand derivative.

To complete the picture the following may be said about the behaviour of $T_F(s)$ for large negative values of s. *P4* and *P8* imply that $T_F(s)$ attains larger and larger positive values as s approaches $-\infty$, but the slope of the curve $y = T_F(s)$ is at no point steeper than -1. Suppose, however, that $E\{X\}$ is finite and let a be the largest number such that $F(s) = 0$ for any $s < a$ (a may be negative infinite), that is $a = \sup\{s \mid F(s) = 0\}$. Then,

A1P9 *If* $E\{X\}$ *exists, then* $T_F(s) \geqq E\{X\} - s$ *with equality for* $s \leqq a$ *and strict inequality for* $s > a$

As a simple example consider the case where X is uniformly distributed over the interval $[0,1]$, that is

$$F(t) = \begin{cases} 0 & t < 0 \\ t & 0 \leqq t < 1 \\ 1 & 1 \leqq t \end{cases}$$

Then, by use of *D1*

$$T_F(s) = \begin{cases} 0.5 - s & s < 0 \\ 0.5(1 - s)^2 & 0 \leqq s < 1 \\ 0 & 1 \leqq s \end{cases}$$

The corresponding curves are illustrated in Figure 1.

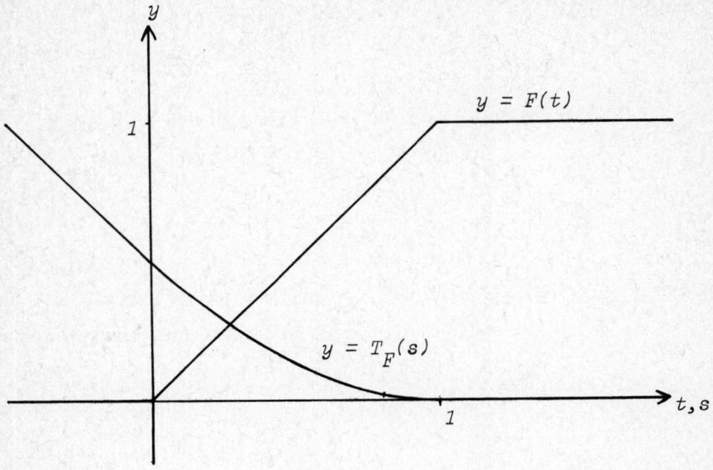

Figure 1 *A uniform distribution function and its transform*

A1.3 T_F AND A SPECIAL CASE OF STOCHASTIC DOMINANCE

Let X and Y be random variables having distribution functions F and G respectively. If $F(t) \leqq G(t)$ for all t, then $1 - F(t) \geqq 1 - G(t)$, that is, $P\{X > t\} \geqq P\{Y > t\}$ for all t. Then F is said to *dominate G stochastically* or, for short, *F dominates G*.

Suppose T_F exists. Then, clearly, T_G exists and $T_F(s) \geqq T_G(s)$ everywhere. Let $F_1, F_2, \ldots, F_n$ be a sequence of distribution functions such that F_k dominates F_{k-1} for $k = n, n-1, \ldots, 2$. Such a sequence is said to be a *monotonic* sequence of distribution functions; if T_{F_n} exists, then so does T_{F_k} for $k < n$ and $T_{F_n}(s) \geqq T_{F_{n-1}}(s) \geqq \ldots \geqq T_{F_1}(s)$ for all s.

In this context a special case of a monotonic sequence of distribution functions plays an important part, namely the sequence $F, F^2, \ldots, F^j \quad j \geq 1$. This sequence arises from the following considerations. Let $Z_j = \max(X_1, X_2, \ldots, X_j)$, where all the X:s are independent random variables having the same distribution function F. Then the distribution function of Z_j becomes $P\{Z_j \leq t\} =$ $= P\{X_1 \leq t \wedge X_2 \leq t \wedge \ldots \wedge X_j \leq t\} = P\{X_1 \leq t\}P\{X_2 \leq t\} \ldots P\{X_j \leq t\} =$ $= [F(t)]^j = F^j(t)$.

If $E\{\max(X,0)\} = E\{X^+\}$ is finite, then so is $E\{\max(Z_j,0)\} = E\{Z_j^+\}$ for any (finite) $j \geq 1$ (since, by definition, $0 \leq Z_j^+ \leq \sum_1^j X_i^+$, which implies $0 \leq E\{Z_j^+\} \leq jE\{X^+\}$). Hence, whenever T_F exists, then so does T_{F^j} and $T_{F^{j+1}}(s) \geq T_{F^j}(s)$ for any (finite) $j \geq 1$. As before, let $a = \sup\{s \mid F(s) = 0\}$ and $b = \inf\{s \mid F(s) = 1\}$. Then

A1P10 *If $a < b$, then for any $j \geq 1$ $\quad T_{F^{j+1}}(s) > T_{F^j}(s)$ for $s < b$ and $T_{F^j}(s) = 0$ for $s \geq b$*

Also in this context it is sometimes necessary to develop integrals like $\int_s^\infty T_{F^j}(t)dF(t)$ for some j. This is done by straight-forward partial integration. Let

$$u = T_{F^j}(t) \qquad v = F(t) - 1$$

$$du = (F^j(t) - 1)dt \qquad dv = dF(t)$$

Then the integral becomes

$$[T_{F^j}(t)(F(t) - 1)]_s^\infty - \int_s^\infty (F^j(t) - 1)(F(t) - 1)dt =$$

$$= T_{F^j}(s)(1 - F(s)) - \int_s^\infty [(1 - F^j(t)) + (1 - F(t)) - (1 - F^{j+1}(t))]dt$$

so that

$$A1P11 \qquad \int_s^\infty T_{F^j}(t)dF(t) = T_{F^{j+1}}(s) - T_{F^j}(s)F(s) - T_F(s) \qquad j \geq 1$$

A1.4 PROOFS

The proofs of these propositions are entirely elementary but are given here for the sake of completeness and easy reference.

P1 was derived in section 1. *P2* and *P3* are immediate consequences of *P4*, *$T_F(s)$ is positive and strictly decreasing for $s < b$ and identically zero for $s \geq b$, where* $b = \inf\{s \mid F(s) = 1\}$, which may be shown by the following argument. Suppose $s < b$. Then $T_F(s) = \int_s^\infty (1 - F(t))dt = \int_s^b (1 - F(t))dt > 0$ in some non-empty open interval containing s. For the same reason $T_F(s+h) - T_F(s) = \int_s^{s+h} (1 - F(t))dt > 0$ for any $h > 0$. Hence, $T_F(s)$ is positive and strictly decreasing for $s < b$.

Suppose $s \geq b$. Then $1 - F(t) = 0$ for all $t > s$ and thus $T_F(s) = 0$ for all $s \geq b$. This completes the proof of *P4*.

P5, *$T_F(s)$ is continuous*, follows from noting that $T_F(s+h) - T_F(s) = \int_s^{s+h} (1 - F(t))dt \to 0$ as $h \to 0$, since $1 - F(t)$ is bounded.

Since $T_F(s)$ is continuous, *P6*, *$T_F(s)$ is convex*, may be reformulated into $T_F(s) \leq (T_F(s-h) + T_F(s+h))/2$ *for all* s *and all* $h > 0$.

This inequality is equivalent to $A \geq 0$ where $A = T_F(s-h) + T_F(s+h) - 2T_F(s) = T_F(s-h) - T_F(s) - (T_F(s) - T_F(s+h)) = \int_{s-h}^{s} (1 - F(t))dt - \int_s^{s+h} (1 - F(t))dt = \int_s^{s+h} F(t)dt - \int_{s-h}^{s} F(t)dt$. Since $F(t)$ is non-negative and non-decreasing, this expression is clearly non-negative, that is $A \geq 0$. Thus the original inequality is true for all s and all $h > 0$.

P7, $T_F(s)$ is differentiable for all s for which $F(s)$ is continuous, follows from noting that $\frac{1}{h}(T_F(s+h) - T_F(s)) = \frac{-1}{h}\int_s^{s+h}(1 - F(t))dt =$ $= -(1 - F(s + \theta h))$ for some θ such that $0 < \theta < 1$ and every[1] $h \neq 0$. Since F is assumed to be continuous at s, this expression tends to the limit $-(1 - F(s))$ as $h \to 0$. Thus $T_F(s)$ is differentiable at s and the value of the derivative is $-(1 - F(s))$. Since F is everywhere right hand continuous the same argument leads to *P8, $T_F(s)$ has a right hand derivative everywhere, the value of which is $-(1 - F(s))$ at the point s.*

P9, if $E\{X\}$ exists, then $T_F(s) \geqq E\{X\} - s$ with equality for $s \leqq a$ and strict inequality for $s > a$, where $a = \sup\{s | F(s) = 0\}$, follows from noting that (see *(A1.1.2)*)

$$E\{X\} \leqq \int_0^\infty (1 - F(t))dt - \int_s^0 F(t)dt = T_F(0) + \int_s^0 (1 - F(t))dt + s = T_F(s) + s$$

where equality holds for $s \leqq a$ and strict inequality for $s > a$.

P10, if $a < b$, then for any $j \geqq 1$, $T_{F^{j+1}}(s) > T_{F^j}(s)$ for $s < b$ and $T_{F^j}(s) = 0$ for $s \geqq b$. Note that

$$T_{F^{j+1}}(s) - T_{F^j}(s) = \int_s^\infty (1 - F^{j+1}(t))dt - \int_s^\infty (1 - F^j(t))dt =$$

$= \int_s^\infty F^j(t)(1 - F(t))dt$ which is clearly strictly positive for $s < b$ and identically zero for $s \geqq b$.

P11 was derived in A1.3. The "straight-forward" partial integration is correct, since $T_{F^j}(t)$ is continuous (by *P5*).

---

[1] sufficiently small

A2 *v* and *u*

A2.1 ASSUMPTIONS AND PROPOSITIONS

Let $c > 0$ be a real number and F a distribution function such that $T_F(0)$ is finite (see *A1D1*). Let q be a real number such that $q = 1/(1+r)$ where $r \geqq 0$, that is, $0 < q \leqq 1$. Define v and u by

A2D1 $\quad$ v *is a real number such that* $T_F(v) = c$

A2D2 $\quad$ u *is a real number such that* $qT_F(u) = c + u(1 - q)$
or, by substituting $1/(1+r)$ *for* q, $T_F(u) = c(1+r) + ur$

Then the following propositions are true:

A2P1 $\quad$ v *is uniquely determined by* $T_F(v) = c$

A2P2 $\quad$ $v \gtreqless 0 \Leftrightarrow T_F(0) - c \gtreqless 0$

A2P3 $\quad$ u *is uniquely determined by* $qT_F(u) = c + u(1-q)$

A2P4 $\quad$ $u \gtreqless 0 \Leftrightarrow qT_F(0) - c \gtreqless 0$

A2P5 $\quad$ $u = v \Leftrightarrow (1-q)(v+c) = 0$

A2P6 $\quad$ $u \in [-c,v]$

A2P7 *u is a strictly decreasing (increasing), continuous function of r, if* $-c < u < v$ $(v < u < -c)$.

A2P8 *u is a strictly decreasing function of c.*

A2.2 PROOFS

P1

By *D1*, v is a solution of the equation $T_F(s) = c$ where $c > 0$. But $T_F(s)$ is continuous (*A1P5*) and takes on any positive value for some $s \in R$. Hence v exists. Moreover, by *A1P4*, T_F^{-1} exists for all positive numbers, so $v = T_F^{-1}(c)$ is unique.

P2

Consider the equation $T_F(s) = c$. By *P1*, $T_F(0) = c \Leftrightarrow v = 0$. By *A1P4*, $T_F(s)$ is strictly decreasing for all s such that $T_F(s) > 0$. Hence $T_F(0) > c \Leftrightarrow T_F(0) > T_F(v) \Leftrightarrow v > 0$, and then also $T_F(0) < c \Leftrightarrow v < 0$, which completes the proof.

P3

By *D2*, u is a solution of the equation

$$(1) \qquad T_F(s) = c(1+r) + sr$$

where $c > 0$ and $r \geqq 0$. By *P1*, only the case $r > 0$ need be examined. The left hand side of *(1)*, $T_F(s)$, is a continuous, non-increasing function mapping R onto the set of non-negative real numbers. The right hand side of *(1)* is a strictly increasing $(r > 0)$ linear function, thus mapping R onto R. Then the difference between the two sides, $T_F(s) - c(1+r) - sr$, is a continuous, strictly decreasing function, mapping R onto R. Hence *(1)* has exactly one solution, that is, u exists and is uniquely determined by *(1)*. *P3* then follows from *D2*.

P4

We found above that the function g given by

(2) $g(s) = T_F(s) - c(1+r) - sr \qquad s \in R$

is continuous and strictly decreasing. Moreover, $g(u) = 0$ and hence $u \gtreqless 0 \Leftrightarrow g(0) \gtreqless 0 \Leftrightarrow qg(0) \gtreqless 0$, where $q > 0$. But $qg(0) = qT_F(0) - c$. *P4* follows.

P5

From the properties of the function g given by (2), it is clear that $g(v) = 0 \Leftrightarrow u = v$. But $g(v) = -r(v+c)$ by (2) and *P1*, and $r = 0$ if and only if $q = 1$. Hence *P5*: $u = v \Leftrightarrow (1-q)(v+c) = 0$.

P6

(i) Suppose $(1-q)(v+c) = 0$. Then $u = v$ by *P5* and hence $u = -c$ $(=v)$ if $v+c = 0$.

(ii) Suppose $(1-q)(v+c) \neq 0$. Then $u \neq v$ by *P5* and $q \neq 1$, that is, $r > 0$. By (2) the equation $g(u) = 0$ may be written as

(3) $T_F(u) - c = r(u+c)$

where $T_F(u) - c \neq 0$ by *P2* since $u \neq v$, and hence $u + c \neq 0$ since $r > 0$. Thus $T_F(u) - c$ and $u+c$ must have the same sign. This occurs if and only if either $(u<v) \wedge (u+c>0)$ or $(u>v) \wedge (u+c<0)$, that is, $-c < u < v$ or $v < u < -c$. Hence, u always belongs to the interval $[-c,v]$.

P7

(i) Suppose $-c < u < v$. By *P3*, (3) and *P1* we may then define the function G by

(4) $r = G(u) = [T_F(u) - T_F(v)]/(u+c)$

where the numerator and the denominator are both positive. G is clearly continuous. Moreover, the numerator is decreasing and the denominator is strictly increasing, so G must be strictly decreasing. Then G^{-1} exists (we knew that already by *P3*) and is continuous. Thus

u is a strictly decreasing continuous function of r if $-c < u < v$.

(ii) Suppose $v < u < -c$. Rewrite *(4)* as

$$(5) \qquad r = G(u) = [T_F(v) - T_F(u)]/[-(u+c)]$$

so that the numerator and the denominator are still both of them positive. The rest of the argument is analogous to the one above.

P8

By *D2*, $c = qT_F(u) - u(1 - q)$. Let H be defined by

$$(6) \qquad H(s) = qT_F(s) - s(1 - q) \qquad s \in R$$

Then $c = H(u)$ and $u = H^{-1}(c)$, so we must show that H^{-1} exists and is strictly decreasing. This follows by noting that

$$(7) \qquad H(s) = qg(s) + c$$

where g, defined by *(2)*, is continuous and strictly decreasing, $q > 0$, and c may be taken to be an arbitrary constant. Hence *P8* (see also Figure 4.3.3).

A3 u_j and v_j

A 3.1 ASSUMPTIONS AND PROPOSITIONS

Let $c > 0$ be a real number and F a distribution function, such that $T_F(0)$ is finite (see *A1D1*). Let q be a real number, such that $q = 1/(1+r)$ where $r \geqq 0$, that is $0 < q \leqq 1$. Define u_j and v_j , $j \geqq 0$, by

$$\text{A3D1}\quad \begin{cases} u_j = \begin{cases} qT_F(0) - c & u_{j-1} \leqq 0 \\ q[u_{j-1} + T_F(u_{j-1})] - c & u_{j-1} > 0 \end{cases} \quad j \geqq 1 \\ u_0 = 0 \end{cases}$$

For $q = 1$, $v_j \equiv u_j$

Then the following propositions are true:

$$\text{A3P1}\qquad u_1 \leqq 0 \Rightarrow u_j = u_1 \qquad j \geqq 1$$

Recall that u is uniquely defined by $qT_F(u) = c + u(1-q)$, (*A2P3*), and $u = v$ for $q = 1$ by *A2P4*.

$$\text{A3P2}\qquad u_1 > 0 \Rightarrow 0 < u \leqq v$$

$$\text{A3P3}\qquad u_1 > 0 \Rightarrow u \geqq u_1 \wedge [u = u_1 \Leftrightarrow F(u-) = 0]$$

A3P4 $u > u_1 > 0 \Rightarrow u > u_j > 0 \qquad j \geqq 1$

A3P5 $u > u_1 > 0 \Rightarrow u_{j+1} - u_j > 0 \qquad j \geqq 0$

A3P6 $u > u_1 > 0 \Rightarrow \lim_{j\to\infty} u_j = u$

A3P7 *The following three expressions are equivalent:*

(i) $u > u_1 > 0$
(ii) $u > \max(0,u_1)$
(iii) $(u > 0) \wedge (F(u-) = 0)$

A3P8 $$\begin{cases} u > \max(0,u_1) \Leftrightarrow u > u_{j+1} > u_j \wedge \lim_{j\to\infty} u_j = u \\ u \leqq \max(0,u_1) \Leftrightarrow u_j = u_1 \end{cases} \qquad j \geqq 1$$

A3P9 $(r > 0) \wedge (v_1 > 0) \Rightarrow u_j < v_j \qquad j \geqq 1$

A3.2 PROOFS

P1

D1 gives $u_j \leqq 0 \Rightarrow u_{j+1} = u_1$ for $j \geqq 1$, so $u_1 \leqq 0$ implies $u_j = u_1$, $j \geqq 0$, by induction.

P2

D1 and *A2P4* give $u_1 > 0 \Leftrightarrow u > 0$ and *A2P6* gives $u > 0 \Rightarrow u \leqq v$. *P2* follows.

P3

By *D1*, *A2P3* and *A1P1*, u_1 may be rewritten as $u_1 = qT_F(0) - c =$
$= qT_F(0) - qT_F(u) + u(1-q) = u - q[u + T_F(u) - T_F(0)] = u - q\int_0^u F(t)dt$.
Suppose $u_1 > 0$. Then $u > 0$ by *P2*. Hence $u - u_1 = q\int_0^u F(t)dt \geqq 0$ with equality if and only if $F(u-) = 0$. *P3* follows.

P4

D1 gives $u_{j+1} = q[u_j^+ + T_F(u_j^+)] - c$ (recall that $x^+ = \max(x,0)$, $x \in R$).

By $A2P3$ we may substitute $qT_F(u) - u(1-q)$ for c to get

$$(1) \qquad u_{j+1} = u - q[(u - u_j^+) - (T_F(u_j^+) - T_F(u))] = u - q\int_{u_j^+}^{u} F(t)dt$$

Suppose $u > u_1 > 0$. Then $F(u-) \neq 0$ by $P3$. Moreover, if $u > u_j > 0$ for some $j \geqq 1$, then $u_{j+1} \geqq u - (u - u_j) = u_j > 0$ by (1) and $u - u_{j+1} = q\int_{u_j}^{u} F(t) > 0$ (since $F(u-) \neq 0$), that is, $u > u_j > 0$ implies $u > u_{j+1} > 0$. But $u > u_1 > 0$ by assumption. Hence $P4$.

P5

Suppose $u > u_1 > 0$. Then $u > u_j > 0$ for $j \geqq 1$ by $P4$ and $F(u-) \leqq F(v) < 1$ by $P2$, $A2P1$, and $A1P4$. Hence (1) gives

$$(2) \qquad u_{j+1} - u_j = (u - u_j) - q\int_{u_j}^{u} F(t)dt \qquad j \geqq 0$$

But $u - u_j \geqq q(u - u_j) > q\int_{u_j}^{u} F(t)dt$ since $u > u_j$ and $F(u-) < 1$, so $u_{j+1} - u_j > 0$. Hence $P5$.

P6

Suppose $u > u_1 > 0$. Then u_j, $j \geqq 1$, is a strictly increasing sequence of positive real numbers, bounded from above ($P4$, $P5$), and hence there exists a unique number α, such that $\lim_{j\to\infty} u_j = \alpha$. By $D1$ and $A1P5$, α must satisfy the equation $\alpha = q[\alpha + T_F(\alpha)] - c$, that is, $qT_F(\alpha) = c + \alpha(1 - q)$. Thus, $\alpha = u$ by $A2P3$. $P6$ follows.

P7

Let A, B, and C denote the expressions

A: $u > u_1 > 0$

B: $u > \max(0, u_1)$

C: $(u > 0) \wedge (F(u-) \neq 0)$

$A \Rightarrow B$ is seen immediately.

$B = [u > 0 \wedge u > u_1] \Rightarrow [u > 0 \wedge u > u_1 > 0] \Rightarrow C$ by *D1*, *A2P4*, and *P3*. Similarly, $C = [u > 0 \wedge F(u-) \neq 0] \Rightarrow [u > 0 \wedge u_1 > 0 \wedge u > u_1] \Rightarrow A$. Hence $A \Leftrightarrow B \Leftrightarrow C$.

P8

By *P7*, $A \Leftrightarrow B$, so by *P4-P6* we have

$$(3) \qquad u > \max(0,u_1) \Rightarrow u > u_{j+1} > u_j \wedge \lim_{j\to\infty} u_j = u \qquad j \geqq 1$$

However, $A \Leftrightarrow C$ as well, so $B' \Leftrightarrow C'$ (A' denotes the negation of A etc), that is, $u \leqq \max(0,u_1) \Leftrightarrow [u \leqq 0 \vee F(u-) = 0]$. Suppose $u \leqq 0$. Then $u_1 \leqq 0$ by *D1* and *A2P4* and hence $u_j = u_1$, $j \geqq 1$, by *P1*. Suppose $u > 0$ and $F(u-) = 0$. Then $u = u_1 > 0$ by *D1*, *A2P4*, and *P3*. Hence $u_j = u_1$, $j \geqq 1$, by *D1*. We conclude:

$$(4) \qquad u \leqq \max(0,u_1) \Rightarrow u_j = u_1 \qquad j \geqq 1$$

Clearly the right hand sides of *(3)* and *(4)* cannot both be true, so we have arrived at a statement of the form $(B \Rightarrow Q) \wedge (B' \Rightarrow R) \wedge (Q \Rightarrow R')$ which is easily seen to imply $B \Rightarrow Q \Rightarrow R' \Rightarrow B$ so that $B \Leftrightarrow Q \Leftrightarrow R'$ and hence $B' \Leftrightarrow Q' \Leftrightarrow R$. *P8* follows.

P9

Suppose $v_1 > 0$ and $r > 0$. Then $T_F(0) > c > 0$ and $q \neq 1$, and hence $v_1 - u_1 = (1 - q)T_F(0) > 0$. *D1* gives

$$(5) \qquad v_{j+1} - u_{j+1} = [v_j^+ + T_F(v_j^+)] - q[u_j^+ + T_F(u_j^+)]$$

Let the function h be defined by

$$(6) \qquad h(s) = s + T_F(s) \qquad s \in R$$

By *A1P5* and *A1P8*, h is seen to be continuous and non-decreasing.

Suppose $v_j > u_j$ for some $j \geqq 1$. We then have

$$(7) \qquad v_{j+1} - u_{j+1} = h(v_j^+) - qh(u_j^+) \geqq (1-q)h(u_j^+) \geqq (1-q)h(0) =$$

$$= (1-q)T_F(0) = v_1 - u_1$$

But $v_1 > u_1$ by assumption. *P9* follows by induction.

A4 $u_j(x)$ and $v_j(x)$

A4.1 ASSUMPTIONS AND PROPOSITIONS

Let $c > 0$ be a real number and Y a random variable having the distribution function F, such that $T_F(0)$ is finite (see *A1D1*). Let q be a real number, such that $q = 1/(1+r)$ where $r \geqq 0$, that is, $0 < q \leqq 1$. Define $u_j(x)$ and $v_j(x)$, $j \geqq 0$, $x \in R$, by

A4D1
$$\begin{cases} u_j(x) = qE\{\max[u_0(\max(Y,x)),\ u_{j-1}(\max(Y,x))]\} - c, & j \geqq 1 \\ u_0(x) = x^+ \end{cases}$$

For $q = 1$, $v_j(x) \equiv u_j(x)$

Then the following propositions are true:

A4P1
$$u_j(x) = \begin{cases} q^j[x^+ + T_{F^j}(x^+) - T_{F^j}(u)] + u(1 - q^j) & x^+ \leqq u \\ q[x^+ + T_F(x^+) - T_F(u)] + u(1 - q) & x^+ > u \end{cases}$$

where u *is uniquely defined by (see A2D2 and A2P3)*

$qT_F(u) = c + u(1 - q)$

(A4P1')
$$v_j(x) = \begin{cases} x^+ + T_{F^j}(x^+) - T_{F^j}(v) & x^+ \leqq v \\ x^+ + T_F(x^+) - T_F(v) & x^+ > v \end{cases}$$

where v *is uniquely defined by (see A2D1 and A2P2)*

$T_F(v) = c$

A4P2 $u_j(x) \gtreqless u_0(x) \Leftrightarrow x^+ \lesseqgtr u$

A4P3 $u_1(x) \leqq u_0(x) \Rightarrow u_j(x) \equiv u_1(x) \qquad j \geqq 1$

A4P4 $u_1(x) > u_0(x) \Rightarrow u \geqq u_1(x) \wedge [u = u_1(x) \Leftrightarrow F(u-)=0]$ (cf A3P3)

A4P5 *The following three expressions are equivalent:*

(i) $u > u_1(x) > u_0(x)$
(ii) $u > \max(u_0(x), u_1(x))$
(iii) $x^+ < u \wedge F(u-) \neq 0$

A4P6 $u > u_1(x) > u_0(x) \Rightarrow u - u_j(x) > 0 \qquad j \geqq 0$ (cf A3P4)

A4P7 $u > u_1(x) > u_0(x) \Rightarrow u_{j+1}(x) - u_j(x) > 0 \qquad j \geqq 0$ (cf A3P5)

A4P8 $u > u_1(x) > u_0(x) \Rightarrow \lim_{j\to\infty} u_j(x) = u$ (cf A3P6)

A4P9
$$\begin{cases} u > \max(u_0(x), u_1(x)) \Leftrightarrow u > u_{j+1}(x) > u_j(x) \wedge \lim_{j\to\infty} u_j(x) = u \\ u \leqq \max(u_0(x), u_1(x)) \Leftrightarrow u_j(x) = u_1(x) \qquad j \geqq 1 \end{cases}$$

A4P10 $-c \leqq u_j(x) \leqq v_j(x) \wedge [(r > 0) \wedge (F(0) < 1) \Rightarrow u_j(x) < v_j(x)]$

$j \geqq 1,\ x \in R$

A4.2 PROOFS

P1

The proof proceeds by induction on j. For $j = 1$, *D1* yields $u_1(x) = qE\{\max(Y,x^+)\} - c = q[x^+ + T_F(x^+)] - c$ and substituting $qT_F(u) - u(1 - q)$ for c one gets

$$(1) \qquad u_1(x) = q[x^+ + T_F(x^+) - T_F(u)] + u(1 - q)$$

so *P1* is true for $j = 1$ and all x.

The basic recursive relation of *D1* can be rewritten as

$$u_{j+1}(x) = qE\{\max[\max(Y,x^+),\ u_j(\max(Y,x))]\} - c =$$

$$\underbrace{qE\{\max[u_j(\max(Y,x)) - \max(Y,x^+)\ ,\ 0]\}}_{Z} + \underbrace{qE\{\max(Y,x^+)\} - c}_{u_1(x)}$$

so that

$$(2) \qquad u_{j+1}(x) - u_1(x) = qE\{Z\}$$

where Z is a short-hand notation for the random variable indicated above. Thus,

$$(3) \qquad E\{Z\} = \int_R \max[u_j(\max(t,x)) - \max(t,x^+),\ 0]dF(t)$$

Suppose $P1$ is true for all x for <u>some</u> value of j. By use of *(3)*, *(2)* and *(1)* the following expressions for $u_{j+1}(x)$ will then be seen to hold.

i. The case $x^+ > u$. By *(1)* and the assumption about $P1$:

$$u_j(\max(t,x)) - \max(t,x^+) =$$
$$= (1 - q)[u - \max(t,x^+)] + q[T_F(\max(t,x^+)) - T_F(u)]$$

Since $u < x^+$, this expression is negative. and so the integrand in *(3)* vanishes identically; hence $E\{Z\} = 0$. By *(2)*,

$$(4) \qquad u_{j+1}(x) \equiv u_1(x) \qquad x^+ > u$$

Thus, $P1$ is true for $x^+ > u$ and $j \geqq 1$.

ii. The case $x^+ \leqq u$. By the assumption about $P1$:

$$u_j(\max(t,x)) - \max(t,x^+) =$$
$$= (1 - q^j)[u - \max(t,x^+)] + q^j[T_{F^j}(\max(t,x^+)) - T_{F^j}(u)]$$

where the expressions within straight parentheses always have the same sign (see *A1P4*); they are non-negative *iff* $\max(t,x^+) \leq u$. Let $A_j(t)$ denote the left hand side of the expression above. Since $x^+ \leq u$ in this case, *(3)* can now be written as

$$(5) \qquad E\{Z\} = \int_{-\infty}^{x^+} A_j(t)dF(t) + \int_{x^+}^{u} A_j(t)dF(t)$$

where the first integral is simply $A_j(x^+)F(x^+)$, that is,

$$[(1 - q^j)(u - x^+) + q^j(T_{F^j}(x^+) - T_{F^j}(u))]F(x^+)$$

and where the second integral can be written as

$$(1 - q^j) \int_{x^+}^{u} (u - t)dF(t) + q^j \int_{x^+}^{u} T_{F^j}(t)dF(t) - q^j T_{F^j}(u)[F(u) - F(x^+)]$$

By straight-forward partial integration one gets

$$\int_{x^+}^{u} (u - t)dF(t) = (u - x^+)(1 - F(x^+)) - (T_F(x^+) - T_F(u))$$

and by *A1P11*

$$\int_{x^+}^{u} T_{F^j}(t)dF(t) = T_{F^{j+1}}(x^+) - T_{F^{j+1}}(u) - T_{F^j}(x^+)F(x^+) + T_{F^j}(u)F(u) - \\ - [T_F(x^+) - T_F(u)]$$

After collecting terms one gets

$$(6) \qquad E\{Z\}= q^j[x^+ + T_{F^{j+1}}(x^+) - T_{F^{j+1}}(u) - u] - \\ - [x^+ + T_F(x^+) - T_F(u) - u]$$

which when inserted into *(2)* yields

$$(7) \qquad u_{j+1}(x) - u_1(x) = q^{j+1}[x^+ + T_{F^{j+1}}(x^+) - T_{F^{j+1}}(u)] - \\ - q^{j+1}u - q[x^+ + T_F(x^+) - T_F(u)] + qu$$

Finally, by use of *(1)*, *(7)* can be rewritten as

(8) $$u_{j+1}(x) = q^{j+1}[x^+ + T_{F^{j+1}}(x^+) - T_{F^{j+1}}(u)] + u(1 - q^{j+1})$$

Thus, *P1* is true for $x^+ \leqq u$ and $j \geqq 1$ as well, which completes the proof.

P2

By *P1*, one can write

(9) $$u_j(x) - x^+ = \begin{cases} (u - x^+)(1 - q^j) + q^j[T_{F^j}(x^+) - T_{F^j}(u)] & x^+ \leqq u \\ (u - x^+)(1 - q) + q[T_F(x^+) - T_F(u)] & x^+ > u \end{cases}$$

from which the proposition readily follows by *A1P4* and *A1P5*.

P3

This is an immediate consequence of *P1* and *P2*.

P4

By *P2*, $u_1(x) > u_0(x)$ is equivalent to $x^+ < u$. By *P1*, $u_1(x)$ can be written as $u_1(x) = u - \int_{x^+}^{u} qF(t)dt$. Thus, if $x^+ < u$, then $u - u_1(x) \geqq 0$ with equality <u>*iff*</u> $F(u-) = 0$

P5

Let A, B, and C denote the expressions

A: $u > u_1(x) > u_0(x)$

B: $u > \max(u_0(x), u_1(x))$

C: $x^+ < u \wedge F(u-) \neq 0$

$A \Rightarrow B$ is seen immediately. $B = [u > x^+ \wedge u > u_1(x)] \Rightarrow$

$\Rightarrow [x^+ < u \wedge u > u_1(x) > u_0(x)] \Rightarrow C$ by *P2* and *P4*. Similarly,

$C = [x^+ < u \wedge F(u-) \neq 0] \Rightarrow [u_1(x) > u_0(x) \wedge u > u_1(x)] \Rightarrow A$.

Hence $A \Leftrightarrow B \Leftrightarrow C$.

P6

If A holds, then C holds *(P5)*, so by *P1*,

$u - u_j(x) = \int_{x^+}^{u} q^j F^j(t)dt$ which is then seen to be positive.

P7

Similarly, $u_{j+1}(x) - u_j(x) = \int_{x^+}^{u} q^j F^j(t)(1 - qF(t))dt > 0$.

P8

Similarly, $0 \leqq u - u_j(x) = \int_{x^+}^{u} q^j F^j(t)dt \leqq uF^j(u)$ which tends to zero uniformly in x as j increases, since $0 < F(u) \leqq F(v) < 1$.

P9

By *P5*, $A \Leftrightarrow B$, so by *P6 - 8* we have for $j \geqq 1$

$$(10) \qquad u > \max(u_0(x),\ u_1(x)) \Rightarrow u > u_{j+1}(x) > u_j(x) \wedge \lim_{j\to\infty} u_j(x) = u$$

However, $A \Leftrightarrow C$ as well, so $B' \Leftrightarrow C'$ (A' denotes the negation of A etc), that is, $u \leqq \max(u_0(x),\ u_1(x)) \Leftrightarrow [x^+ \geqq u \ \vee \ F(u-) = 0]$. Then, by *P3*, *P2* and the expression in the proof of *P7* above, we have

$$(11) \qquad u \leqq \max(u_0(x),\ u_1(x)) \Rightarrow u_j(x) = u_1(x) \qquad j \geqq 1$$

Clearly the right hand sides of *(10)* and *(11)* cannot both be true. We have now arrived at a statement of the form $(B \Rightarrow Q) \wedge (B' \Rightarrow R) \wedge (Q \Rightarrow R')$ which is easily seen to imply $B \Rightarrow Q \Rightarrow R' \Rightarrow B$ so that $B \Leftrightarrow Q \Leftrightarrow R'$ and hence $B' \Leftrightarrow Q' \Leftrightarrow R$. *P9* follows.

P10

a. $-c \leqq u_j(x) \leqq v_j(x) \qquad x \in R,\ j \geqq 0$

(i) $v_0(x) = u_0(x) = x^+ > -c$

(ii) Suppose $-c \leqq u_j(x) \leqq v_j(x)$ for some value of j. By *D1*

$v_{j+1}(x) = E\{\max[\max(Y,x^+),\ v_j(\max(Y,x))]\} - c$

and

$$u_{j+1}(x) = qE\{\max[\max(Y,x^+),\ u_j(\max(Y,x))]\} - c \geq -c$$

so that

$$v_{j+1}(x) - u_{j+1}(x) \geq (1-q)E\{\max[\max(Y,x)^+,\ u_j(\max(Y,x))]\} \geq 0.$$

b. $(r > 0) \wedge (F(0) < 1) \Rightarrow u_j(x) < v_j(x) \qquad x \in R,\ j \geq 1$

Suppose $r > 0$ and $F(0) < 1$. Then $q \neq 1$ and $T_F(0) > 0$, and hence (by *P1* and *P1'*) $v_1(x) - u_1(x) = (1-q)(x^+ + T_F(x^+)) \geq (1-q)T_F(0) > 0$ (Cf the proof of *A3P9*.)

Suppose $v_j(x) > u_j(x)$, $x \in R$, for some $j \geq 1$. We then have by *D1*
$$v_{j+1}(x) - u_{j+1}(x) \geq (1-q)E\{\max[\max(Y,x)^+,\ u_j(\max(Y,x))]\} =$$
$$= (1-q)[E\{\max(0,\ u_j(\max(Y,x)) - \max(Y,x^+))\} + E\{\max(Y,x^+)\}] =$$
$$= (1-q)\ E\{\max(0,\ u_j(\max(Y,x)) - \max(Y,x^+))\} + (1-q)(x^+ + T_F(x^+)) > 0$$
But $v_1(x) > u_1(x)$ by assumption. *P10* follows by induction.

A5 $u_j(x)$ and $v_j(x)$ in the More General Case

A5.1 ASSUMPTIONS AND PROPOSITIONS

Let c_j, $j \geqq 1$, be a sequence of positive real numbers and Y a random variable having the distribution function F, such that $T_F(0)$ is finite (see *A1D1*). Let q be a real number such that $q = 1/(1+r)$ where $r \geqq 0$, that is, $0 < q \leqq 1$. Define $u_j(x)$ and $v_j(x)$, $j \geqq 0$, $x \in R$, by

A5D1
$$\begin{cases} u_j(x) = -c_j + qE\{\max[u_0(\max(Y,x)),\ u_{j-1}(\max(Y,x))]\},\ j \geqq 1 \\ u_0(x) = x^+ \end{cases}$$

For $q = 1$, $v_j(x) \equiv u_j(x)$

The following notation will be used in order to simplify the form of the explicit expressions for $u_j(x)$ and $v_j(x)$:

A5D2 $\quad$ b_{jk} *is a solution of*

$$q^k T_{F^k}(b_{jk}) - (1 - q^k) b_{jk} = c_j +$$
$$+ q^k [T_{F^k}(b_{j-1\ k-1}) + b_{j-1\ k-1}] -$$
$$- q[T_F(b_{j-1\ k-1}) + b_{j-1\ k-1}],\ 1 \leqq k \leqq j$$

$b_{j0} = 0$ *for* $j \geqq 0$ *and* $b_{jk} = 0$ *for* $k > j$

For $q = 1$, $a_{jk} \equiv b_{jk}$

A5D3 E_{jk} *is the subset of the real line that satisfies*

$$E_{j+1\ 1} = \bigcup_{k=1}^{j} [E_{jk} \cap \{x|x^+ > b_{jk}\}]$$

$$E_{j+1\ k+1} = E_{jk} \cap \{x|x^+ \leqq b_{jk}\} \qquad 1 \leqq k \leqq j$$

$$E_{11} = R$$

For $q = 1$, $D_{jk} \equiv E_{jk}$

Then the following propositions are true:

A5P1 b_{jk} *is uniquely defined by* $D2$

A5P2 $$u_j(x) = x^+ + q^k[T_{F^k}(x^+) - T_{F^k}(b_{jk})] + (1 - q^k)(b_{jk} - x^+) \qquad x \in E_{jk}\ ,\ 1 \leqq k \leqq j$$

A5P2' $$v_j(x) = x^+ + T_{F^k}(x^+) - T_{F^k}(a_{jk}) \qquad x \in D_{jk}\ ,\ 1 \leqq k \leqq j$$

A5P3 $$-c_j \leqq u_j(x) \leqq v_j(x) \qquad x \in R\ ,\ j \geqq 1$$

A5.2 PROOFS

P1 By $D2$, $b_{j0} \equiv 0$ and $b_{jk} = 0$ for $k > j$. For $1 \leqq k \leqq j$, b_{jk} can be determined recursively starting from $b_{j-k\ 0} = 0$. It is seen from $D2$ that the recursion proceeds diagonally down the matrix formed by the b_{jk}:s that is, b_{jk} determines $b_{j+1\ k+1}$ and so on.

Suppose $b_{j-1\ k-1}$ exists uniquely for some value of j and k. This is certainly true for $k = 1$ and any $j \geqq 1$. Then b_{jk} must satisfy the equation

$$(1) \qquad q^k T_{F^k}(b_{jk}) - (1 - q^k) b_{jk} = y$$

where y is a well-defined real number.

For $q = 1$ (1) becomes $T_{F^k}(b_{jk}) = y'$ is positive by *A1P10*. This determines $b_{jk} (= a_{jk})$ uniquely by *A2P2*. For $q = 0$ we get $b_{jk} = -c_j$.

Suppose $0 < q < 1$. To establish the existence and uniqueness of b_{jk} it is sufficient to show that the left hand side of (1) is a continuous, strictly monotonic function of b_{jk}, mapping R onto R. This means that the left hand side of (1) takes on any given value for one and only one value of b_{jk}.

Let $g(z) = q^k T_{F^k}(z) - (1 - q^k)z$ so that $g(b_{jk}) = y$. We want to show that g is a continuous, strictly monotonic mapping of R onto R. g is clearly continuous (*A1P5*). Its right hand derivative exists everywhere (*A1P8*):

$$g'(z+0) = q^k(F^k(z) - 1) - (1 - q^k) = q^k F^k(z) - 1$$

$g'(z+0)$ is negative, so g is strictly monotonic (decreasing). Finally, $g(z) \to -\infty$ as $z \to \infty$, for $T_{F^k}(z) \to 0$ as $z \to \infty$ by *A1P4*, and for $z < 0$, $g(z) > q^k T_{F^k}(0) - (1 - q^k)z \to \infty$ as $z \to -\infty$. Thus, g maps R onto R.

So, by induction, b_{jk} is uniquely defined by *D2*.

P2

We want to show that

$$P2 \qquad u_j(x) = x^+ + q^k[T_{F^k}(x^+) - T_{F^k}(b_{jk})] + (1 - q^k)(b_{jk} - x^+)$$

$$x \in E_{jk}, \quad 1 \leqq k \leqq j$$

is the solution of the difference equation given in *D1*; b_{jk} and E_{jk} are defined by *D2* and *D3*.

The proof proceeds by induction on j. For $j = 1$ *D1* yields $u_1(x) = -c_1 + qE\{\max(Y, x^+)\} = -c_1 + q[T_F(x^+) + x^+]$ and substituting

$qT_F(b_{11}) - (1 - q)b_{11}$ for c_1 (by *D2*), one gets

$$(2) \qquad u_1(x) - x^+ = q[T_F(x^+) - T_F(b_{11})] + (1 - q)(b_{11} - x^+)$$

$$x \in E_{11} = R$$

so *P2* is true for $j = 1$.

The basic recursive relation of *D1* can be rewritten as
$u_{j+1}(x) = -c_{j+1} + qE\{\max[\max(Y,x^+), u_j(\max(Y,x))]\} =$

$$= qE\{\max(Y,x^+)\} + qE\{\underbrace{\max[u_j(\max(Y.x)) - \max(Y.x^+), 0]}_{Z}\} - c_{j+1}$$

so that

$$(3) \qquad u_{j+1}(x) - x^+ = qE\{Z\} + qT_F(x^+) - (1 - q)x^+ - c_{j+1}$$

where Z denotes the random variable indicated above. Thus,

$$(4) \qquad E\{Z\} = \int_R \max[u_j(\max(t,x)) - \max(t,x^+), 0]dF(t)$$

Suppose *P2* is true for some value of j. By use of *(4)*, *(3)* and *(2)* the following expression for $u_{j+1}(x)$ will then be seen to hold.

(i) We start by developing *(4)* for $x \in E_{jk}$ for some k such that $1 \leqq k \leqq j$ (where j is now a fixed number such that *P2* is true), and get

$$(5) \qquad E\{Z\} = \int_R \max\big(0, q^k[T_{F^k}(\max(t,x^+)) - T_{F^k}(b_{jk})] + $$
$$+ (1 - q^k)[b_{jk} - \max(t.x^+)]\big)dF(t) =$$
$$= \int_{-\infty}^{x^+} \max\big(0, q^k[T_{F^k}(x^+) - T_{F^k}(b_{jk})] + (1 - q^k)(b_{jk} - x^+)\big)dF(t) +$$
$$+ \int_{x^+}^{\infty} \max\big(0, q^k[T_{F^k}(t) - T_{F^k}(b_{jk})] + (1 - q^k)(b_{jk} - t)\big)dF(t)$$

(ii) Consider the case $x \in E_{jk} \wedge \{x|x^+ > b_{jk}\}$. Then $E\{Z\} = 0$ by *(5)*,

so that by *(3)*, $u_{j+1}(x) - x^+ = -c_{j+1} + qT_F(x^+) - (1-q)x^+$ and by substituting $qT_F(b_{j+1\ 1}) - (1-q)b_{j+1}$ for c_{j+1} (by *D2*) we get

$$(6) \qquad u_{j+1}(x) - x^+ = q[T_F(x^+) - T_F(b_{j+1\ 1})] + (1-q)(b_{j+1\ 1} - x^+)$$

for $x \in E_{jk} \wedge \{x|x^+ > b_{jk}\}$ for <u>any</u> k such that $1 \leqq k \leqq j$. Thus, *(6)* holds for $x \in \bigcup_{k=1}^{j} [E_{jk} \wedge \{x|x^+ > b_{jk}\}] = E_{j+1\ 1}$ (see *D3*). By induction *P2* is seen to hold for $x \in E_{j1}$ for any $j \geqq 1$.

(iii) Consider the case $x \in E_{jk} \wedge \{x|x^+ \leqq b_{jk}\} = E_{j+1\ k+1}$. We then get by *(5)*

$$E\{Z\} = F(x^+)[q^k[T_{F^k}(x^+) - T_{F^k}(b_{jk})] + (1-q^k)(b_{jk} - x^+)] +$$
$$+ q^k \int_{x^+}^{b_{jk}} T_{F^k}(t)dF(t) - q^k T_{F^k}(b_{jk})[F(b_{jk}) - F(x^+)] +$$
$$+ (1-q^k)b_{jk}[F(b_{jk}) - F(x^+)] - (1-q^k)\int_{x^+}^{b_{jk}} t dF(t)$$

But, by *(A1P11)*

$$\int_{x^+}^{b_{jk}} T_{F^k}(t)dF(t) = [T_{F^{k+1}}(x^+) - T_{F^{k+1}}(b_{jk})] - T_{F^k}(x^+)F(x^+) +$$
$$+ T_{F^k}(b_{jk})F(b_{jk}) - [T_F(x^+) - T_F(b_{jk})]$$

and by straight-forward partial integration

$$\int_{x^+}^{b_{jk}} t dF(t) = b_{jk}F(b_{jk}) - x^+F(x^+) + [T_F(x^+) - T_F(b_{jk})] - (b_{jk} - x^+)$$

Putting things together we get

$$(7) \qquad E\{Z\} = q^k[T_{F^{k+1}}(x^+) - T_{F^{k+1}}(b_{jk})] -$$
$$- [T_F(x^+) - T_F(b_{jk})] + (1-q^k)(b_{jk} - x^+)$$

Next, substitute the expression for c_{j+1} given by (see *D2*)

$$q^{k+1}T_{F^{k+1}}(b_{j+1\ k+1}) - (1 - q^{k+1})b_{j+1\ k+1} =$$

$$= c_{j+1} + q^{k+1}[T_{F^{k+1}}(b_{jk}) + b_{jk}] - q[T_F(b_{jk}) + b_{jk}]$$

for c_{j+1} in *(3)* to get

$$(8)\qquad u_{j+1}(x) - x^+ = qE\{Z\} + qT_F(x^+) - (1 - q)x^+ - q^{k+1}T_{F^{k+1}}(b_{j+1\ k+1}) + (1 - q^{k+1})b_{j+1\ k+1} + q^{k+1}[T_{F^{k+1}}(b_{jk}) + b_{jk}] - q[T_F(b_{jk}) + b_{jk}]$$

Finally. inserting the expression for $E\{Z\}$, given by *(7)*, into *(8)* and collecting terms. we get

$$(9)\qquad u_{j+1}(x) - x^+ = q^{k+1}[T_{F^{k+1}}(x^+) - T_{F^{k+1}}(b_{j+1\ k+1})] + (1 - q^{k+1})(b_{j+1\ k+1} - x^+)$$

for $x \in E_{jk} \cap \{x | x^+ \leqq b_{jk}\} = E_{j+1\ k+1}$ for <u>any</u> k such that $1 \leqq k \leqq j$.

By induction *P2* is seen to hold.

P2'

is an immediate consequence of *D1* - *D3* if q is set equal to *1* in *P2*.

P3

(i) $-c_1 \leqq u_1(x) \leqq v_1(x)$ by *A4P10*.

(ii) Suppose $-c_j \leqq u_j(x) \leqq v_j(x)$ for some value of j. Then $-c_{j+1} \leqq u_{j+1}(x) \leqq v_{j+1}(x)$ as well, which is seen by substituting c_{j+1} for c in the corresponding part of the proof of *A4P10*. *P5* follows by induction.

References

BAUMOL W J (1966). Economic models and mathematics. In: *The Structure of Economic Science* (ed. by Krupp), pp 88-101. Prentice-Hall, Englewood Cliffs, N.J.

BREIMAN L (1964). Stopping-rule problems. In: *Applied Combinatorial Mathematics* (ed. by Beckenbach), pp 284-319. Wiley, New York.

BROWN T A (1967). Another optimal stopping problem. Paper P-3635. The RAND Corporation, Santa Monica, California.

BUNGE M (1962). *Intuition and Science*. Prentice-Hall, Englewood Cliffs, N.J.

BUNGE M (1967). *Scientific Research, Vol. 1 - The Search for System.* Springer-Verlag, Berlin.

DeGROOT M H (1968). Some problems of optimal stopping. *Journal of the Royal Statistical Society, Series B, 30*, 108-122.

DeGROOT M H (1969). Sequential statistical decisions and optimal stopping. Paper presented at the Scandinavian - GSIA Joint Faculty Seminar, Lerum, Sweden. Printed in: *Behavioral Approaches to Modern Management, Vol. 1* (ed. by Goldberg). Gothenburg Studies in Business Administration, Gothenburg, 1970.

DeGROOT M H (1970). *Optimal Statistical Decisions*. McGraw-Hill, New York.

ELFVING G (1967). A persistency problem connected with a point process. *Journal of Applied Probability 4*, 77-89.

HAYES R H (1969). Optimal strategies for divestiture. *Operations Research 17*, 292-310.

HESS S W (1962). A dynamic programming approach to R and D budgeting and project selection. *IRE Transactions on Engineering Management, EM-9*, 170-179.

KARLIN S (1962). Stochastic models and optimal policy for selling an asset. In: *Studies in Applied Probability and Management Science* (ed. by Arrow, Karlin, Scarf), pp 148-158. Stanford University Press, Stanford.

McCALL J J (1965). The economics of information and optimal stopping rules. *Journal of Business 38*, 300-317.

MacQUEEN J and MILLER R G Jr (1960). Optimal persistence policies. *Operations Research 8*, 362-380.

MacQUEEN J B (1964). Optimal policies for a class of search and evaluation problems. *Management Science 10*, 746-759.

MARCH J G and SIMON H A (1958). *Organizations*. Wiley, New York.

MARSCHAK T and YAHAV J A (1966). The sequential selection of approaches to a task. *Management Science 12*, 627-647.

RADNER R (1964). Mathematical specification of goals for decision problems. In: *Human Judgements and Optimality* (ed. by Shelly II and Bryan), pp 178-215. Wiley, New York.

RAIFFA H and SCHLAIFER R (1961). *Applied Statistical Decision Theory*. Division of Research, Graduate School of Business Administration, Harvard University, Boston. (Paperback edition: M.I.T. Press, Cambridge, Mass., (1968).)

RAIFFA H (1968). *Decision Analysis*. Addison-Wesley, Reading, Mass.

SAKAGUCHI M (1961). Dynamic programming of some sequential sample design. *Journal of Mathematical Analysis and Applications 2*, 446-466.

SIMON H A (1965). Mathematical constructions in social science. In Braybrooke, *Philosophical Problems of the Social Sciences*, pp 83-98. MacMillan, London.

STAËL von HOLSTEIN C.-A. S (1970). *Assessment and evaluation of subjective probability distributions*. The Economic Research Institute at the Stockholm School of Economics, Stockholm.

TUCKER H G (1962). *An Introduction to Probability and Mathematical Statistics*. Academic Press, New York.